The 1000 Things Projects

The 1000 Things Projects:

*Counting Your Way
to a Healthier Relationship
with Your Stuff*

by John Sener

Copyright ©2022 John Sener
All rights reserved

No part of this book may be reproduced, or stored in a retrieval system, or transmitted in any form or by any means, electronic, mechanical, photocopying, recording, or otherwise, without express written permission of the publisher.

ISBN: 978-0-578-35771-3
Cover design by: John Sener
Printed in the United States of America

Table of Contents

Part I: Getting Started — 1
- You and Your Stuff: Time for a Talk about Your Relationship? — 2
- Beyond Clutter Control — 7
- Getting Started — 12

Part II: Holding On — 21
- Stories — 22
- Inner Voices — 28
- Treasures — 37
- Possession — 47

Part III: Letting Go — 59
- Curation — 60
- Gratitude — 74
- Slow on the Inflow — 84
- The Results — 89

Part IV: Getting Better, Getting Good — 99
- Starting a Second Project — 100
- Learning from Others — 106
- Tuning in to Healthy Talk — 114
- Culling as Habit: Tackling the Tough Stuff — 122
- Throwing Your Life Away: Letting Go of the Tougher Stuff — 132
- Appreciation: The Healthiest Habit — 141

Part V: Getting Personal — 149
- Building a Long-Term Healthy Relationship...and Beyond — 150

Acknowledgements — 161

Notes — 163

Appendix: Chart of Strategies — 177

Part I: Getting Started

You and Your Stuff: Time for a Talk about Your Relationship?

So, how's that relationship of yours going these days? You know, that relationship with the stuff you own. The one that's filled with all this amazing stuff that makes your life so much nicer... except for that other stuff that's stressing you out or getting in your way. The one that seems healthy enough most of the time... except when it feels like what you own is owning you instead. The one where some things mean so much, and it's so hard to let some things go, but maybe the relationship with some of them could be... over? Or at least better?

Oh, you're in a relationship all right, even if you haven't been paying attention to it. If you need a reminder, just pick a room in your house, start throwing out all the things in that room, and see what happens. Maybe they will start disappearing into the trash without a second thought. More likely, something will slow you down and stop you. That "something" is your relationship with your stuff. It's the one with the voices in your mind telling you what to keep and why through messages like these: 'But I have to keep this juicer; I might use it again someday. Oh, and that waffle iron too. And the wok with the missing handle — I shouldn't just throw it out; I can probably still use it.' Or messages like this one: 'I paid a lot for that treadmill; it's probably still worth something — I can't just give it away,' Yeah, that relationship.

Everyone has a relationship with their stuff. It's a curious one when you think about it. In some ways, it's a lot like being in a relationship with a person — the conversations, the negotiations, and especially the attachments. These attachments are often so strong: 'Well, of course we need to keep Grandma's dining room table; it meant so much to her.' In fact, sometimes these relationships are even stronger than your relationships with people — more durable, longer lasting, more emotional even. After all, relationships with people come and go, but Grandma's dining room table stays with you, just as surely as your memories of Grandma herself. It's the same with lots of other things you have all over your house and perhaps beyond: your closets, your basement, your attic, your spare room, your garage, your storage unit(s). Your relationship with your stuff may not really be as important as your relationships with the people in your life, but the attachments are just as real: Grandma's dining room table... the sea shell collections from those beach vacations 10, 20, 30 years ago... the pile of T-shirts from college... that threadbare, shredded pillow your mother made... and so on. Your particular list of stuff will be different, but that's the point: your relationship with your stuff is important as a physical embodiment of you and your life. It's personal.

Despite all that, you may have been taking this relationship for granted, at least until now. Chances are, you're reading this book because you're feeling less than satisfied about the relationship, and you're trying to figure out what to do about it. You might be someone who:

- Wants to change something about this relationship, even if you're not quite sure what that is.
- Lives in a home which has too many areas that feel like a cluttered, dysfunctional mess.
- Is downsizing or empty nesting as part of a process of changing how you live, such as moving to a new dwelling or aging with intention.
- Wants to find a way to stop the seemingly relentless accumulation of stuff that is threatening to overwhelm your living space.
- Feels that the amount of stuff you own is not healthy for you, your life, or the planet.

- Simply wants a healthier relationship with your stuff.

It might be time to ask yourself what's *really* going on between you and the things that surround you. In my case, I decided it was time to have a talk with my stuff about our relationship. I already knew that we were having some of the same issues you might be having: Why do I still have so much stuff? Why is it so hard to let go of things? What is it all doing in my life, anyway?

Having this talk with myself inspired me to launch a project to get rid of 1,000 things from my house, which I did over an eight-month period. Clearing my house of clutter was important to me, but I also wanted to move beyond simple decluttering. I wanted to be *thoughtful* about exploring my relationship with my stuff and its hold on me. I didn't start out thinking that I needed to build a healthier relationship with my stuff in the process, but that's where I ended up. The Talk was the beginning of a journey to find some answers to my questions — a journey something like one you might be ready to take.

Why I Wrote This Book

The "1,000 Things Project" started out as a purely personal, solitary endeavor; I was several months into the project before I even told anyone else about it. When I started mentioning the project to a few friends and colleagues as a topic of conversation, I expected them to treat my project as more of a curiosity than anything, or perhaps as a sign that I was suffering from an early onset of eccentricity. Instead, their reactions took me by surprise:

> "I *have to* start doing that."
> "That is *such* a good idea."
> "I have been thinking about your project and mentioned it to some friends again yesterday."
> "I'm going to start doing that -- today!"

The reactions were immediate, forcefully expressed, even visceral. My friends and colleagues expressed their intentions to do something, and then in later conversations they would tell me what they had done. This surprised me even more because I never recommended the idea or tried to push it on anyone, and I certainly never thought of it as a movement or a cause. I wasn't trying to get anyone to do anything; I was just trying to make conversation.

After this happened several times, I started bringing up the topic on purpose to see how people would react, and a lot of people were eager to talk. It was as if the phrase 'the 1,000 Things Project' was a call to action for clear and obvious reasons that they immediately understood. A few of them said that they had also been having conversations with their stuff.

Maybe you feel a similar need to change how you relate to the stuff you own. Maybe you feel that you have too many things in your home that affect your life in some negative ways, and maybe you want to do something about it. So I wrote this book to share with you how doing a 1,000 Things Project helped me build a healthier relationship with my stuff and how doing your own 1,000 Things Project can do the same for you. The book is organized into five main parts:

- **Getting Started** explains the process I used to begin my project, which you can use to help you get started on yours;
- **Holding On** is about the attachments to things that you may discover along the way as I did;
- **Letting Go** describes strategies for freeing yourself from your attachments to your things;
- **Getting Better, Getting Good** details how to get better at letting go of your stuff by becoming more strategic about the process; and
- **Getting Personal** talks about how to build a long-term healthy relationship with your stuff.

At the end of most chapters is a section called "Your Turn" because this book is designed to help you build a healthier relationship with your stuff in whatever way makes sense for you. You'll find lots of strategies, lessons learned, and suggestions; their purpose is to help you direct your own journey, not to prescribe what your journey should be. You can do a 1,000 Things Project however you like. Here's how I did mine.

Beyond Clutter Control

Before the 1,000 Things Project, my relationship with my stuff was in a place that may sound familiar to you. I enjoyed having many of the things that I owned, but it bothered me that so much of my house was a cluttered mess. It was filled with more stuff than I really wanted, yet I also had a strange feeling that something much more important was *missing*. I wanted things to be different; something needed to change.

The messy clutter in my home had persisted despite my best efforts. I'd been doing clutter control for many years, and I had gotten pretty good at it in some ways. I'd given away several large pieces of furniture to family members, and I'd recycled reams of office documents. I had a Clutter Control folder in my e-mailbox and a Clutter Control bookmark folder on my web browser. I had even hired a professional organizer who helped me to reduce my clutter while teaching me plenty of useful tips in the process. I had learned how to group and organize my stuff to find new homes for it, and I had gotten much better at using a scanner to reduce the clutter of papers in my home office. I had developed plans and schemes for getting rid of this stash or cleaning out that corner of a room.

All of this was helpful, and my home was noticeably more organized and less cluttered. Even so, my home office was still littered with bins and boxes, and my file cabinets still held hundreds of folders. There were collections of things nested all over the house in corners and closets and drawers; some of these collections had a discernible reason for being there, others not so much. All in all, my clutter control efforts weren't taking me to where I wanted to be, and truth be told, I wasn't really sure where that was. I had made plenty of progress, but progress toward what? My decluttering started to feel more like puttering. Doing more of the same wasn't doing it for me anymore.

Then a curious idea emerged, more of a notion, really: what would it be like to live in a home where I could look at every thing I owned and know why I owned it?

My first reaction to this idea was that it was a bit ridiculous — you mean, *every* thing? Clearly the things I knew I wanted to have and keep, such as things I valued as keepsakes or used every day, were not an issue. The problem was with all those *other* things in my home whose purpose and value were not at all clear to me. There were things I hadn't used or worn or looked at for years or even decades … things in boxes I hadn't opened since the last time I'd moved … kitchen drawers stuffed with various utensils that I never used anymore and in some cases had forgotten how … a box with four bottles of "boiler colloid" for the boiler that had been replaced the previous year … a Hawaiian shirt residing in my clothes closet with other shirts waiting in vain to be worn again.

The prospect of going through all these things to determine their purpose or value made the idea feel like an impractical, almost nonsensical notion. But what if I made it a goal anyway and tried to reach it by getting rid of a lot of things? Maybe a large, round number of them? That might not get me all the way there, but maybe trying would get me close enough to know whether this goal really was attainable or simply some hopeless pipe dream. At least trying to reach this goal would make my house look and feel better.

So, I got out a piece of legal-size paper and wrote these words at the top of the page: "Clutter control: get rid of 1000 items in 238 days." My intention was to complete the project by the end of the calendar year, December 31. I used the familiar label "clutter control" because I didn't have a name yet for what I was really doing. But this headline wasn't really telling the whole story. Wanting to know the purpose or value of all my things reflected a desire to move beyond simply getting rid of stuff, or tidying up, or feeling organized. This goal may have seemed impossibly remote, but it meant that the 1,000 Things Project would be more than just another clutter-control effort on a larger scale.

Setting this goal got me to thinking about what else I wanted, what was missing, and where I wanted to be. Two experiences in particular influenced my thoughts. One was the experience of having recently become a solo empty nester, which suggested possibilities for change: downsizing a lot more, possibly moving to a new place, maybe even to a new city. Contemplating these possibilities didn't make me feel freer, though. Instead, it made me feel weighed down and a bit trapped by my possessions, especially by the prospect of having to move so many of them again. I still remembered the ordeal of my last move, which involved around 130 boxes of stuff, plus all the things that weren't in boxes, even after getting rid of about 20 percent of my stuff. Eight years later, it seemed like I had about the same amount of stuff again. The more things I had, the more difficult it would be to move them, so it was a bit unsettling to realize that my stuff would have such a large say in any decision I might make when the time came.

The other was the experience of helping to clear out my parents' house after both of them had passed away. For more than a year, my sisters and I, along with various other family members, spent hours upon hours sorting through thousands of objects, filling dumpsters, and finding unexpected stashes and "treasures" at every turn. At times it felt like we were engaged in battle with my parents' stuff — room to room, drawer to drawer, box to box and jar to jar combat. What possessed my parents to keep so many things? Why did they leave such a jumbled hoard behind? What were they thinking? I didn't really know, but I was sure that I didn't want to end up in the same place as they had; in fact, this was a big reason I'd started doing clutter control in the first place.

Both of these experiences reminded me that the things we own are far more than just inert objects. How else to explain the hold that my parents' stuff had on them? My relationship with my own stuff was also more complicated than simply deciding what to toss and what to keep. In fact, it felt as if I was in a relationship with my stuff. How else to explain the hold that my things had on me? This relationship was certainly not where

I wanted it to be; it may not have been as unhealthy or as limiting as my parents' relationship with their stuff had seemed to be, but the similarities were disturbing. I needed to get a handle on the things I owned and to restore a sense of balance and control, so I decided that establishing a *healthier* relationship with my stuff would be another goal of my project.

Pursuing this goal would move me even farther beyond clutter control, but to get there, I would have to do some things differently. I would need to have a serious discussion to figure out what was going on between me and my stuff. It was time for The Talk.

The Talk

Things, it's time you and I had a little talk about our relationship.

I looked around at my things and started asking them lots of questions. Things, why are there so many of you? What am I going to do with all of you? What keeps me so attached to you? How did you get here in the first place? Why are you still here? What's stopping me from letting go of you? What are you doing in my life? For my life? To my life?

Having a conversation like this may sound odd, but it was a way of acknowledging that my relationship with my stuff was more than just a conversation with myself. My things didn't have lives of their own exactly, but they did have their own meanings beyond the ones I gave them, such as the particular purpose for which they were made or the meanings that others would give them before, after, or even while I owned them. Talking directly to my things helped me give them the consideration and respect they deserved as the other party in our relationship.

At first, my things didn't have much to say in reply, although that would change soon enough. Even so, having The Talk gave me a few initial answers to some of my questions. One reason that my house held so many things was because I had collected them effortlessly and thoughtlessly for many years. The days of young adulthood when I'd possessed far fewer things were now in a rather distant past. Homeownership, the passage of time, and raising a child had produced a gradual accumulation of material things. I could afford them, so it took relatively little effort or thought to acquire them. They entered my household in a steady, seemingly endless flow, and eventually there was too much stuff to pay attention to all of it. My clutter control efforts fell short of what I needed because decluttering by itself was a relatively thoughtless process compared to identifying the purpose or value of all my belongings.

Pursuing this goal would require me to pay attention and to be thoughtful about the process. These are important elements of a healthy relationship with a person, so it made sense that paying attention and being thoughtful would also help me build a healthier relationship with my stuff. Being environmentally responsible was also important; I didn't want to pass the buck by throwing lots of stuff in the garbage or just dumping it off at a thrift store. As a result, I decided to do the 1,000 Things Project thoughtfully and responsibly by setting ground rules for the project that meant something to me, by keeping track of each thing I got rid of, and by paying attention to what happened along the way.

Goals

The Talk helped me clarify my goals for doing the 1,000 Things Project:

- Make my house look and feel noticeably less cluttered;
- Gain insights into my attachment to things, both in general and relative to specific objects;
- Do the process as responsibly and thoughtfully as possible;
- Establish a healthy(ier) relationship with my stuff; and
- Make progress toward an ultimate goal to live in a home where I can identify the purpose or value of everything I own.

With those goals in mind, my 1,000 Things Project began.

Getting Started

The first step in getting the project going was to set some ground rules, starting with making a list to keep track of things.

Keeping Track: The List

This part was simple. On the piece of legal-size paper where I'd written "Clutter control: get rid of 1000 items in 238 days," I kept a list of everything I got rid of in numerical order. Throughout this book, any numbered object refers to one of those things -- for example, #1 was a golf training aid, and #65 was a cat litter box. Each thing was also coded according to how I got rid of it by using the following categories:

> R = Recycle
> D = Donation
> G = Gift
> F = Freecycle
> T = Trash
> T/R = partly Trashed, partly Recycled

Recycle (R) -- Some things (most commonly shredded documents and other forms of paper, as well as plastic and metal objects) were completely recycled by putting them in recycling bins for curbside collection, while other things were partly recycled and partly trashed (T/R); for example, there were many badges and lanyards from conferences (for instance, #427-466), for which I recycled the paper badge but threw out the plastic part and usually the lanyard itself.

Donation (D) -- Charities and thrift stores were the most common recipients of donations. Some charities offered home pickup service, while other donations found their way into collection bins and book-sharing boxes located nearby. Although I noted where many of the donated items went (see the Results chapter for more details), I did not track charity recipients closely since this was not a project goal. Also, I did not seek a tax credit for any of the items I donated except for a car (#153) since changes in US tax laws made it much more bothersome to determine the value of donated items, and accumulating tax credits was not one of my project goals either.

Gift (G) -- At times, I gave a thing directly to someone when I knew they would like it or use it.

Freecycle (F) -- Freecycle is part recycling, part giving; it's a way to recycle your things by giving them to people in your local community. Freecycling involves joining a local member group online. Freecycle has thousands of groups with millions of members around the world. To sign up online, go to https://www.freecycle.org/ and find out if there is a Freecycle group in your community.

Trash (T) -- This was generally an option of last resort, to be used only if I couldn't find a better way to get rid of something.

What Is a "Thing"?

Counting things required me to define what a "thing" was, which wasn't as straightforward as you might think. How to count a pair of something? A box of something? A folder full of papers?

Being thoughtful about the process gave me an answer. It took a fair amount of time, energy, and attention to look at each single object thoughtfully and decide what to do with it, and this requirement seemed more important than whether something was a separate, physical object. As a result, my definition of a thing was *anything that required my time, energy, or attention as an individual, separate entity*. Using this definition, I developed a personalized, if somewhat idiosyncratic, set of criteria to determine what was a thing. For example:

- A pair of anything (shoes, gloves, socks, dice, etc.) counted as one thing because I could deal with them as one block of time, energy, and attention and make one decision.
- A box or bag of something counted as one thing if I could deal with it as one thing, and it counted as separate things if I had to consider each item separately. For example, one glance at a bag of some small plastic objects told me that none of them were worth keeping, so that bag counted as one thing (#91; trashed), while several old tins of shoe polish (#418-421; trashed) counted as separate things because I had to go through them one by one to sort out the good ones from the bad ones.
- Size didn't matter. When I donated my 2000 Honda Accord (#153), for example, the car and everything I left in it counted as one thing, because I only had to deal with it as one thing. However, when I threw out a road map that I'd salvaged from the car (#130), that also counted as one thing, because that particular road map required my time, energy, and attention to decide what to do with it.
- I also grouped things together to make one thing. For example, there was a large collection of pencils, pens, and other writing utensils which had accumulated over the years; I had to sort through all of them, but I didn't really need to pay attention to each individual pencil or marker. Instead, I sorted them into five bags by type (lead pencils, colored pencils, pens, markers, and crayons; #66-70) and posted them on Freecycle, where they quickly found takers.
- Papers were the hardest thing to define. It seemed crazy to consider each piece of paper in my office as a single thing, even though I often had to look at each sheet to decide what to do with it. As a compromise, I decided to use folders or digital files as my unit of "thingness" for papers; each folder I emptied or culled counted as one

thing, or each digital file that I created from a folder of papers counted as one thing.
- Identifying an item as being ready to go was not enough; it had to be gone from the house before it was counted as part of the 1,000 things and recorded on the list.
- A thing had to be a physical object or set of objects. One could do a similar project with digital or other non-physical things, like a credit card account or an email account, but I did not do that for this project, although I kept it in mind as a possible future project.
- I didn't count consumables, such as discarded packaging, empty bottles or cans or tubes of toothpaste, because I wanted the 1,000 Things Project to be about things I was otherwise holding on to, not about things I was already getting rid of in the everyday flow of my life. I made a few exceptions to this rule with things that had been around for so long that they were no longer consumable, for instance some bottles of expired vitamins, fish oil capsules, and electrolyte tablets (#386-388; trashed).

It was not easy to follow this definition and the related criteria exactly every time, and there were also occasional gray areas, which showed how defining "thingness" was a very personal decision. For example, early in the project I counted seven pairs of shoes as 14 things (#34-47; donated), partly because I had to sort through a large bin of shoes to match them up. On the other hand, road maps (#111-119, 130; recycled) always counted as single things even when I found them in bunches; each of them required individual attention because they were especially important to me, partly because I still had a collection of hundreds of them from my childhood.

Ultimately, what mattered was that my particular way of defining a "thing" worked for me. When anyone asked me how to define a thing, my response was always that they should feel free to define a "thing" in any way that made sense for them. (When one person asked me, "Can I count my ex as a thing?" my reply was, "You can count him for as many things as you like.")

Why Count to 1,000?

Deciding to count to 1,000 came naturally to me as someone who likes to count things and has a bit of a clerical streak. It also provided a clear numerical target and an easy, structured way to measure progress over time. Still, it's fair to ask, why choose 1,000 and not some other number? After all, the number 1,000 is an arbitrary one to some extent, an accident of biology and math; we use a base 10 numbering system because we have 10 fingers and 10 toes. One reason for choosing 1,000 was that reaching most of my goals would require a fairly large number. Another reason was simply that, like many people, Large Round Numbers appeal to me. So 100 was clearly too small, although a "100 things project" could be a way to get started on such a journey more easily.

I decided not to do a "net flow" project, that is, to remove 1,000 more things than I acquired, because I wanted to focus on learning from the experience of getting rid of things. Besides, keeping track of things leaving the house would be enough work without also keeping track of things coming into the house.

There was another, more philosophical reason for selecting 1,000. I'd always been intrigued by the Tao concept of the "Ten Thousand Things," which for me captured how the myriad of things in the material world threatens to overwhelm us by their sheer numbers and blind us to the deeper truths of existence. In other words, too much stuff keeps us from seeing what's really important. While in theory at least, we can have as many things as we want so long as we can recognize the Tao in each and every one of them, in practice this is really, really hard to do. Observing hoarders and clearing out my parents' house taught me how overwhelming physical possessions can be. As a result, I found myself wondering how my own belongings might have overwhelmed me without really being aware of it. Would getting rid of 1,000 things make me feel less burdened by the multitude of physical objects in my home, my personal "Ten Thousand Things"? To get from 10,000 to 1,000, I applied the concept of tithing, which is generally defined as a voluntary contribution of one-tenth of one's annual income to support a church or clergy. My adaptation of this definition was to get rid of one-tenth of my worldly goods to serve a higher set of purposes, including greater self-insight, charity, and a healthier life in some way. That may have been a far more roundabout way to arrive at 1,000 than was necessary, but again the important thing was that having this source of motivation worked for me.

Why a "Project"?

Calling it a project helped to remind me that this endeavor would require paying attention to my target timeline, doing a little planning now and then, and being willing to adapt along the way. Naming it as a project also supported my goal of doing the process as responsibly and thoughtfully as possible. It's actually pretty easy to get rid of 1,000 things once you put your mind to it. An afternoon or two of going through a garage or basement or attic, assembling a pile of stuff, and then calling a junk hauler to take it away requires some effort, but not necessarily a lot of thought. *Adding a sense of thoughtfulness or stewardship changes the process completely.* Placing a value on each object, deciding what to do with it, and then caring what happens to it, all takes more effort and commitment. Doing the 1,000 Things Project as an extended act of thoughtful stewardship also seemed likely to support my other goals, so it would be well worth the time and effort.

The Start: The Surge and the Slog

The project started with an initial surge, thanks to a number of items already assembled from previous clutter control efforts. On the first day I got rid of two dozen things, including several golf training aids (#1-4) and a bunch of binders (#5-24), all on Freecycle. The golf training aids (putting cup, putting pal, swing groover, and golf journal) were all somewhat old but barely or never used. Over the next few days, I got rid of more things on Freecycle, including a couple of watches (#30, 31), a balance ball chair (#64), and an extra cat litter pan (#65) which had become surplus to requirements when our household had downsized from two cats to one who spent most of his time outdoors. I also donated some shorts and shoes (#33-47) and trashed a few things such as a bag of old screws (#26) and a box that I couldn't recycle (#32).

A total of 65 things were gone after one week, and in the first month I got rid of a total of 283 things — more than one-quarter of the way there! This initial surge was highlighted by a huge push in early June that included the largest object I donated (my old car) and my largest donation in numerical terms (129 things to Vietnam Veterans of America, consisting mainly of old clothes; #154-246). The project was off to a roaring start, and some changes were already apparent. A few places in the house seemed less cluttered, which made me feel lighter and more spacious. Getting rid of my second car and a few other really big things gave me a sense of relief. Even better, almost everything on the list was donated, Freecycled, or recycled, so I was doing the process responsibly and thoughtfully. Surely I would be able to reach my target well before my self-imposed deadline of December 31 -- maybe even far ahead of schedule.

This optimism turned out to be premature. During the summer, my momentum waned, and the initial burst of energy slowed to a slog. It took me nearly another four months, into early October, to get halfway to my goal, and eventually I fell behind schedule.

What happened? Like races and romances, the slowdown was inevitable to some extent; my opening burst of enthusiasm settled into a slower, steadier pace. After going through my initial stash of items targeted for disposal, it took longer to identify new ones. Life also intruded, scattering my energy and attention both literally and figuratively all over the map, as I took nearly a dozen trips for both business and pleasure, went on summer vacation, and indulged in various other diversions.

Although my focus naturally drifted during this period, this summertime slowdown also had a deeper, more important source. As I paid thoughtful attention to removing things from my life, they returned the favor by revealing the sources of their attachments to me and showing me how these attachments made it much harder to part with them. It turned out that my stuff had a lot to say after all, so I started to listen more closely, and that was when the project really got started.

Your Turn: Getting Started with Your Project

Doing a 1,000 Things Project is a self-starter for many people. Maybe you are one of them; all you needed was to read the words "1,000 things," and you were ready to go. If so, good for you! Feel free to use this book as a guide; most chapters will have a Your Turn section at the end with exercises to help you, and you can also look at the strategies chart in the Appendix and try some of them out along the way.

If you're just getting started, here are a few quick tips to get your project off to a great start:

Pick a target number that means something to you. Having a specific target number makes it easier to imagine yourself finishing the project once you've started it. Of course, 1,000 is a fine number, but you can choose a different number if that's more appropriate for you.

Give your project a name. Call it "My 1,000 Things Project" if you like, or call it something else that motivates and engages you: "My Best Spring Cleaning Ever," "Me and My Stuff," "The New Me," or whatever has meaning for you. Naming your project personalizes it, gives it an identity, and creates buy-in and ownership in the process.

Start with easy stuff. Choose a single item that you already know you don't want or need, or start with an area that really bothers you. Or, pick a type of thing, for instance clothing or toiletries or kitchenware, and start sorting through them.

Do It Your Way. This tip is the most important one. A 1,000 Things Project is more than DIY (Do It Yourself); it's DIYW (Do It Your Way). Review the process described in this chapter for some ideas on how to structure your project. Have a talk with yourself if that would help you; ask yourself what you want to accomplish by doing a 1,000 Things Project, and set goals for yourself based on that talk. Set a timeline and decide how you're going to keep track of your progress.

Having trouble getting started? *You already have.* After all, if you've read this far, you've already spent some time, energy, and attention on getting started. Why not begin the project itself by getting rid of a few things and see where it goes? Picking the exact right object or place is not important; just start somewhere, whenever you like: right now, while you're reading this book, or after you finish the book.

Part II: Holding On

Stories

You might imagine the process of sorting through your stuff to be a quiet, solitary activity, but in fact, once you start paying thoughtful attention to your things, the process becomes more like a chatterbox of conversation. Getting this conversation started is easy; simply look at an object you own, think about what it means to you, and then just listen. Usually, that will be enough for you to discover that your stuff has a lot to say.

One of the main reasons that your things have a lot to tell you is that *every thing we own has a story*. Our lives are filled with stories, and many of these stories are attached to our stuff. Paying thoughtful attention to our things brings these stories to life and reveals a lot about the sources of our attachments to our belongings.

My home was as filled with stories as it was with stuff. Many of my things were difficult to get rid of because they evoked stories that were based on fond memories or reminiscences. For instance, parting with my collection of old license plates was really difficult because looking at any one of them caused memories to emerge as if from a hiding place. Many times I looked at those license plates thinking, *Time to recycle these*, and I found myself remembering some fond moment instead. When I actually started trying to put them in a metal recycling bin one by one, holding each plate transported me on an extended ride down memory lane: memories of the car(s) the plate was on, memories of living in that state at that time, stories of love and marriage and fun weekend excursions and of lives past, my own and others. The only way I could persuade myself to put the license plates into the bin was to take pictures of them and to tell myself that the pictures would evoke the memories just as powerfully as the actual metal objects did. Even then, for a moment I balked at my decision and considered alternative fates for them. Maybe my license plates could be put to some creative use more worthy of their past service. Maybe they could go on a bar wall or perhaps a mailbox. One of the LittleFreeLibrary structures in my town was decorated with license plates, so maybe I could build one like that and put it in my yard. Eventually the doubts passed as I realized that having the pictures was good enough, so in the metal recycling bin they stayed until they went off to the recycling center (#570-579).

I didn't always take the time to recall the story behind every thing, but the stories were there for the telling, even if it was a small anecdote. For instance, throwing out some old leftover Christmas wrapping paper scraps (#106) conjured brief memories of presents wrapped, opened, and appreciated, of smiles, surprises, and seasonal tidings of comfort and joy. Even if a thing was easy to get rid of, such as an old pair of worn-out Birkenstocks (#411; trashed) with many miles of memories trod into them, or some spelling and math books (#74-75; recycled) from my son's elementary school days, it often required a moment to reminisce before I could let it go.

Naturally, most of these stories reflected the meanings that these objects had for me, but some of my things had their own secret stories that had little or nothing to do with me. There was an old basketball so worn that it no longer had any grip (#587; trashed), which my son had used and the neighborhood kids had borrowed sometimes to shoot baskets at our hoop on the street next to the end of the driveway. There was a pair of old rollerblades with the wheels missing (#93; trashed) which carried my son on little adventures I will never know about. There were old eyeglasses (#389-394; donated) worn by my father at various stages of his life. Although I didn't know the stories, I knew that they were there, and it was fun to imagine what they might have been.

Sometimes my things told stories about their origin, use, or the meanings they might have after I owned them. For instance, going through a stash of pencils and other assorted writing tools reminded me of an article that I'd read in my hometown newspaper when I was a kid about the geographic origins of the pencil. The story had fascinated me then, and I'd thought about it now and again throughout my adult years. The article explained how a pencil was manufactured with materials that came literally from around the world: graphite from Brazil or Mexico, wood from California or Sweden or South Africa, rubber from Thailand or Malaysia, paint from Kazakhstan or Estonia. Remembering this story reminded me that even the humblest of objects could have truly remarkable stories of origin. Collectively, the constituent parts in my collection of pencils had traveled mind-boggling distances to enter my home, and it was humbling to realize that my pencils were more well-traveled than I was. Thinking about their stories of origin gave me a newfound respect for the pencils and other writing tools in my collection. As I assembled them in bags and sent them on their way to continue their journey (#53-63, 66-70; Freecycled), I wondered what their future stories might be. What doodles or documents or art works would they be used to make, and what stories would they help create in the process?

Accumulating lots of stuff means accumulating lots of stories. Paying attention to these stories while sorting through my stuff made me realize that I had become a collector of both, which also reminded me of my parents and their own penchant for collecting things.

The Christmas Tree Story

My parents had a lot of stuff. They were like many people of their generation who'd had the good fortune to grow old and gradually prosper in a home where they lived for several decades. Whenever my siblings and I visited my parents, we couldn't help but notice how their home changed over the years. Rooms that once functioned as rooms gradually became storage spaces; empty floor space eventually turned into narrow paths or disappeared entirely under solid piles of stuff. Tables, desks, countertops, and most other horizontal surfaces became useless except for holding the things placed upon them.

As we started coming to grips with their mortality during their later years, my siblings and I tried to help them deal with how their stuff was affecting their quality of life. We were also starting to wonder how we were going to deal with their stuff once they had passed. Although we could see for quite some time what we were going to be up against, we couldn't do all that much about it. Sometimes our parents would cooperate with our efforts to help them organize their belongings, but more often they would forcefully resist those efforts, and we never knew which way they were going to be on any given visit.

The first time this really hit home for me involved dealing with their Christmas trees. My parents had bought live Christmas trees for many years, and they'd even planted one on their property, a magnificent blue spruce which graced a corner of their front yard and grew to be over thirty feet tall. But their interest in live trees had long since past, and my parents had started using artificial Christmas trees instead.

Convenience may have been their intent, but that's not how it worked in practice. I learned this during a visit one early December when my mom asked me to go up to the attic and bring the Christmas tree down for them. My sisters had warned me that the attic was a cluttered mess, but my parents said that finding the tree would be easy because they stored their Christmas items right next to the opening of the dining room closet entry to the attic. This closet had built-in steps leading up to the attic, so storing Christmas items there enabled my dad to stand on the closet steps to retrieve them without having to crawl around in the attic itself.

Or at least that was how it was supposed to work. In practice, I went up into the attic and looked in every box and bag near the opening, but I could not find the artificial Christmas tree. I crawled on my hands and knees through a small path in the attic between the dining room closet entry and the other entry point over the garage and looked at every box along the way, but I couldn't find anything there either. Regrettably, I went back down to the living room and told my mom I couldn't find the tree. She thanked me for trying and then went out later and bought a new one.

The next year, I visited at about the same time, and again my mom asked me to go up in the attic to get the "new" artificial Christmas tree, so I did. This time I found the tree without any problem. Then I also found the tree I'd been looking for the previous year. This got me curious, so I kept looking around, and I eventually found *seven* artificial Christmas trees. To this day, I have no idea why I could find no trees one year and so many trees the next. After I brought down the tree that my mom wanted, she inspected it and then noticed that a piece was missing. Although it wasn't clear whether or not the piece was actually necessary, I offered to go up and get another Christmas tree, but the damage had already been done. She thanked me again for my efforts, and then after I left, she -- you guessed it -- went out and bought another artificial Christmas tree.

This experience taught me that my parents were collectors, but I didn't really understand then how deeply their collections would affect me. That was a lesson I was to learn Some Day.

In dealing with my own stuff, I learned that being thoughtful about how I got rid of my things revealed their stories, no matter how small or seemingly trivial the things were. Some of these things, such as my collection of license plates, were hard to get rid of because they embodied stories that attached them to me. These stories revealed the more personal relationship I had with these things by evoking memories and other meanings that expressed my identity and sense of self. The stories explained to me the purpose or value of my things, or at least what that purpose or value once was. Other times, my things told me stories that were independent of any personal meanings I might give to them. These stories were based on the journeys my things took to arrive in my possession or on the roles they played in someone else's life.

Paying attention to these stories slowed down my decision-making process, but it was so rewarding to recall or discover them that the extra time and effort were well worth it. At the same time, something else was also slowing down the process that the stories themselves couldn't explain. I could understand why it was difficult to decide what to do with things that had personal meaning for me, but why did I hold on to that battery charger for so long? And why was it so difficult to decide what to do with so much of the other stuff? The answers to those questions reflected another, different source of attachments.

✽✽✽✽✽✽✽✽✽✽✽✽✽

Your Turn: Listening to Stories of Your Stuff

1) **Listen to Stories of Your Stuff.** What stories do your things have to tell you? Pick a random object in your home. It could be a thing you've decided to get rid of, a thing you're trying to decide whether to keep or let go, or a thing that has particular meaning or value to you. Take a moment to look at that object and just listen to whatever stories emerge.

2) **Identify your attachments.** What attachments do the stories reveal? Identify the kind(s) of attachments you have to that object after listening to the story or stories it tells you. Are they:

   - Memories, reminiscences, remembrances of people, places, and experiences you've had?
   - Values which are important to you?
   - Intentions of future purpose or use?
   - Some other kind of attachment(s)?

3) **Capture a story.** Write down one or more of the stories you hear as the result of paying attention to a thing you own.

Inner Voices

Stories are only one source of the internal dialogue you will hear when you go through your stuff with thoughtful attention. Stories can tell you a lot about your attachments to the objects you encounter, but they won't tell you what to do with those objects. Sometimes, stories about the personal meaning of some items may influence your decisions about what to do with them, but the stories themselves don't make the decisions. As I learned from listening more closely to my stuff, these decisions came from an entirely different source: an ensemble of inner voices that were not just making suggestions about what to do; they were running the show.

Scripts and Mantras

Going through my stuff responsibly meant trying to make a thoughtful decision about every single object I encountered. Sometimes these decisions were easy, such as Freecycling a set of training wheels (#48-49; counted as two things because they had been separated) which I knew I would never use again. It was a no-brainer to throw away various objects that were in a smelly bag and couldn't be used anymore (#82-90). It was a pleasure to give away a children's book illustrated by a friend (#95) as a present to my niece's daughter.

Most decisions about what to do with stuff were not so easy because they provoked resistance. For instance, Freecycling a Yakima Powerhound ski rack attachment (#28) required having a lengthy internal dialogue about whether or not to give it away. It was many years old, never used, and it didn't fit on my new car. But it was still new, so maybe it was worth something. Eventually, I decided that trying to sell it wasn't worth the effort, so I gave it away instead. Freecycling a balance ball chair (#64) involved a similar conversation: I'd paid a fair amount of money for it, and I hadn't used it much. So should I give it away or try to use it more often first? Again, I decided it wasn't worth the effort to use it more frequently, so I gave it away.

Deciding to get rid of an old bike carrier rack (#152; Freecycled) generated even more resistance. The bike rack had given me long and reliable service on my old car, but it didn't fit on the new car I'd bought the year before. I had no intention of using the old car to transport bicycles anymore, but the old bike rack stayed anyway. Maybe I'd need to transport many bikes using two cars. (Very unlikely.) Maybe I'd want the old rack in case my new car broke down and I needed to use the old car. (Even more unlikely.) Maybe I could get some money for it. (More than 12 years old and all beat up? Totally unlikely.) It was almost as if, after all those years of being attached to the old car, the bike rack had gotten, well, attached to that old car, and it wasn't going to leave until the car did, which is what happened.

Where was this resistance coming from? The relationship between my old car and my old bike rack may have been a nice story, but that story did not really explain why it was so hard to let go of the bike rack. As I paid closer attention, I began to hear the other voices involved in the conversation, the ones talking about money and possible future use and what to do just in case something happened, however unlikely that something might be. These voices were telling me reasons for holding on to my things. They communicated with me in the form of scripts — short but powerful instructions intended to guide my decisions about what to do with my things. These scripts were voiced in phrases that reflected basic beliefs I held about how to value things in various material, financial, sentimental, or practical ways. They had been running unnoticed in the background of my mind like automatic programs until I started paying attention to them. Here are some of the most common ones I encountered:

- 'It might be worth something; I can't just throw it out.'
- 'I paid a lot for that; I can't just give it away — maybe I can get some money for it.'
- 'My [name of relative or other person] might want that someday.'
- 'This was my favorite [thing] when I was a kid.'
- 'I might want to look through those (papers, pictures, drawings, etc.) someday.'
- 'This was so-and-so's favorite [thing].'

Just as every thing I owned had a story to tell, almost every thing I'd owned for any appreciable length of time had a script which emerged whenever I was deciding what to do with that object. Most of these scripts explained my attachments to those things and the underlying resistance to getting rid of them. Old running shirts: *'Maybe you can still use them.'* Um, no; they weren't even good enough to keep as rags (#383-384; trashed). Conference tote bags: *'These are still useful; you can't just throw them away.'* Um, OK, you have a point there (#636-665; donated). An outdoor canopy chair: *'You paid a fair amount of money for that, and it's such a clever design, and you like it so much. You can't just throw it away.'* But the chair seat was ripped and beyond repair, and my seat nearly hit the ground the last time I tried to sit in the chair. So yes, I could just throw it away (#671; trashed), even while regretting that I'd left it outside so much and wishing I had taken better care of it.

There were a few scripts which actually made it easier to get rid of things. For instance, *'When it's used up, throw it away or recycle responsibly'* made it easy to get rid of things like empty printer cartridges (#71, #287-299; recycled). *'It's broken; throw it away'* was an even simpler disposal script for broken items, such as a set of non-working ear phones, a pair of broken sunglasses, and a broken toy part (#123, #710, #750; all trashed). *'This is too old/gross to use anymore! Get rid of it'* was useful for things that weren't entirely empty but couldn't be used anymore, such as old toiletries or cleaning supplies (#370-380, #413-417, #590-598, #606-635; trashed/recycled). Occasionally, an object had no script at all because I couldn't figure out why I had kept the thing, such as a metal name plate (#539; recycled) or a tea bag thing (#309; trashed). No script meant no attachment, so disposing of those items was easy.

The process of listening to these scripts became an integral part of the 1,000 Things Project. Being thoughtful changed the process from a monologue into a conversation. Once I started paying attention to these inner voices and their scripts, my decision-making switched from automatic to manual. As I became more practiced at hearing these scripts and challenging their directions, more specific rules underlying the scripts often emerged, such as *'Don't waste anything!' 'Get your money's worth!'* or *'Remember who you are and where you came from!'* Some of these rules appeared in multiple scripts; for instance, *'Get your money's worth!'* was the rule underlying *It might be worth something; I can't just throw it out* and *I paid a lot for that; I can't just give it away,* among others. The rules themselves formed patterns, which I found myself calling "mantras" because they expressed my basic beliefs and often repeated themselves. After a while, I started naming some of them. The first mantra I named was Maximum Value. This mantra embodied positive virtues of economy and thrift (*'Don't waste anything!' 'Get your money's worth!'*) but sometimes also went to extremes (for example, *'Always get the lowest price!'*). It's that mantra that makes us drive an extra few miles to save a penny or two on a gallon of gas even when it really costs more time and energy to do so. I never actually heard an inner voice saying *Maximum Value;* it was a label for a pattern of scripts and rules that I often heard. But there were other mantras whose names I had heard often and for quite some time.

Some Day and Just in Case

My parents' house also had inner voices. Some of these voices are familiar to anyone whose parents grew up during the Great Depression. Sometimes these became outer voices as well through the stories my parents told about their experiences. My mom told us many stories about her life during the Depression, especially about her family's poverty and deprivation -- how often they ate squirrel or other game for dinner, how they made their own clothes, or how she wore nothing but hand-me-downs since she was the younger sister. Curiously, even though my dad loved to tell stories about all sorts of things, he almost never talked about his experience as a child during the Depression.

The memories of my mom's stories still echo in my mind, but the easiest place to hear these echoes of the Great Depression was in our parents' house. Collections of multiple items filled their home, and their stockpile of artificial Christmas trees was only one example of their tendencies to have multiples of things. We didn't really understand how serious this was until the day arrived when we found ourselves clearing out the mounds of collections they had accumulated: eight artificial Christmas trees, seven or more toolboxes, six shelves of junk-filled coffee cans, five bins of metal, four broken appliances, three lawn tractors, two unneeded cars... It was as if the Twelve Days of Christmas had horribly mutated into the Twelve Years of Clutter — although in their case, it was more like fifty years' worth.

Many of the scripts and mantras I encountered during The 1,000 Things Project were also echoes of the Depression. They were internalized rules and messages about how to deal with things based on lessons learned from my parents while I was growing up. My parents in turn had learned these lessons from their much harsher childhood experiences.

Two other mantras that echoed my parents' Depression experience were easy to name since I often heard them during my project. Some Day was about the notion that a day would come when anything one saved would be useful or valuable: '*I might be able to use that (again) Some Day,*' '*[Someone] might want to look at those (again) Some Day.*' A close companion to this mantra, which I called Just in Case, was based on the need to be prepared for emergencies or other unforeseen contingencies. In my parents' case, Just in Case was about more than just simple preparation:

'Better keep a few dozen tissue boxes in the closet Just in Case.' 'Save those toolboxes/jars of bolts/scraps of metal Just in Case we need them Some Day.' My parents' house was filled with Just in Cases whose purpose was to help them avoid want and deprivation by being prepared for the worst. Some Day and Just in Case explained the urge to hold on to things tightly: 'We might need that Some Day. You never know. Better hold on to it Just in Case.' Some Day also reflected the inevitability which results because things endure. My parents never used most of the stuff they had saved, but Some Day arrived anyway when they passed and their things remained.

Some Day and Just in Case had another source besides my parents' Depression experience. My parents' house also echoed their experiences of World War II. My dad never told stories about World War II either, at least not until the last few weeks before his passing. We knew the general outline of his story: born in March 1927, he turned 18 in 1945, was drafted, and had to leave his first year of college to go to war. He was put on a troop ship and sent to Italy, but by the time he arrived there, the war was over. There was no fighting to be done, although he stayed for several months touring the country doing some duties whose purpose he never clearly explained. During his life, we'd often thought that this was the epitome of good fortune, and I had wondered more than once whether I owed my very existence to this timing. When we went through our parents' belongings after their passing, however, a far darker reality emerged. We found a chest filled with memorabilia from the war, and we sorted through some letters and personal effects. Then we came across some pictures taken in the piazza of a small town somewhere in Italy, but they were nothing like the touristic pleasures of Italian piazzas that we'd experienced during our visits. These pictures showed the grisly reality of post-war Italy: corpses of Mussolini supporters with ropes around their necks and hung in the town square for all to see. I suddenly understood why my father hated traveling so much and especially abroad. Imagine being torn out of one's college and professional life path to be put in uniform, shipped across the ocean, and have little to do but travel around and see the gruesome aftermath of war, the gore without glory. It was no wonder that he never wanted to talk about it.

I came to believe that the emerging consumerism of post-World War II American society offered my parents a certain solace and distance from the struggles of the Great Depression and the war. Collecting things formed a comforting layer of insulation that may have helped remove them from the hardships that had formed and defined their lives. Their version of Just in Case was about keeping things as a way of making sure that they never had to experience that level of deprivation again. They didn't talk about these hardships very often, but their stories spoke loud and clear to us through their collections of belongings, and they were especially loud when Some Day finally arrived and we had to decide what to do with all the things they had left behind.

Meta-Talk, Negative Self-Talk

Most of my internal dialogue was focused on my relationship with individual things, but there were also inner voices focused on my relationship with the project itself. Some of this meta-talk was positive and affirmed the progress I was making toward my goals: *'Forty-four things today! That's a good day's work.' 'The corner of this room looks a lot less cluttered now.' 'Over 60 things this week! That'll help me get caught up.'* Some of the meta-talk was more about describing or improving the process: *'Up to 487 things so far — almost halfway there.' 'About time I threw those things out.' 'Falling behind schedule; try to pick up the pace.'*

Unfortunately, not all of the meta-talk was constructive; an inner critic often emerged whose messages added to the internal resistance I encountered. Sometimes this inner critic's negative self-talk was aimed at undermining the project itself: *'This is a waste of time. This is not worth the effort. Why are you being such a stickler about this?'* Other self-defeating thoughts were aimed directly at myself: *'People will think you're really weird for doing this. You **are** really weird for doing this. What **is** wrong with you* *anyway?'* These negative messages persisted throughout the project; they didn't stop me, but they did slow the process down at times.

Most of this negative self-talk was not particularly novel either, but occasionally my inner critic would come up with something that was rather original or even entertaining. A particular favorite was one I encountered soon after starting the project: *'Getting rid of your stuff is un-American.'* That one caught my attention, partly because it seemed that wanting to have much less stuff, rather than accumulating as much as possible, *did* feel faintly un-American. It prompted me to wonder about the possible effects of shutting down this never-ending flow of consumer products through my life. What would happen if everyone aspired to own only things whose purpose and value they could identify? Would the economy collapse? *'Maybe American society as we know it would become extinct?'* That last question was a bit dramatic, but you know how self-talk can be. I respectfully disagreed with the notion that my 1,000 Things Project was unpatriotic, but the underlying question about the relationship between the project and affluence remained in the background, unresolved for quite some time.

Paying attention to the inner voices I heard was an important step toward building a healthier relationship with my stuff. Scripts, mantras, and other inner voices explained why it often felt so hard to get rid of things thoughtfully and responsibly. The stories my things shared with me revealed why I held on to things and what their purpose or value was to me. Scripts and mantras usually directed me to keep things, which meant that getting rid of things often took a lot of effort because making such decisions required deviating from the script. Meta-talk helped keep me engaged in the process, and even negative self-talk challenged me to confront my inner critic's negative messages and put them in their place. Listening to these inner voices also helped me understand why my relationship with my stuff was so important and valuable -- even something to treasure.

✳ ✳ ✳ ✳ ✳ ✳ ✳ ✳ ✳ ✳ ✳ ✳ ✳

Your Turn: Your Inner Voices

1) **Your Scripts.** Use the table below to list one or more of the scripts that you hear most often or which seem most important to you when you're making decisions about your stuff. Use the examples in the Scripts and Mantras section of this chapter as prompts. If your scripts are similar but have different wording, write down your version(s).

2) **Your Mantras.** Do the same thing with your mantras. What are your most basic beliefs for deciding what to do with your stuff? What specific rules or patterns repeat themselves when you're dealing with your stuff? List the one(s) which you often or are important to you, using the examples in the Scripts and Mantras section of this chapter as prompts. List your mantra(s) using your name(s) for them.

3) **Your Meta-Talk and Negative Self-Talk.** Identify at least one 'meta-talk' message (*'That's a good day's work.' 'That'll help me get caught up.'*) and one 'negative self-talk' message (*'This is a waste of time. This is not worth the effort.'*) that you hear in your mind when you are deciding what to do with some of your things. Use the examples in the Meta-Talk, Negative Self-Talk section of this chapter as prompts.

Type of Inner Voice	Examples of Inner Voices You Hear
Your Script(s)	
Your Mantra(s)	
Your Meta-Talk	
Your Negative Self-Talk	
[add your own type]	

Treasures

Your relationship with your stuff takes another step forward when you realize that sorting through your stuff is about more than just getting rid of things.

We also have good reasons for holding on to many of the things we have. As you sort through your stuff, eventually you will encounter things that have special meaning to you. These things are more than just useful or practical or even valuable; they are things that you treasure. The purpose and value of these belongings is that they give you a sense of belonging. Your treasures might be collections of things that embody your sense of identity and self, or they might be heirlooms that connect you to your family history or to a larger history, or they might be other keepsakes that evoke cherished memories of past relationships, journeys, or other experiences.

The process of identifying your treasures with thoughtful attention changes the experience of sorting through your stuff. Identifying my treasures added a new dimension to my 1,000 Things Project, which now also became an exploration of my personal treasure trove, the "store of valuable or delightful things" in my home. Some of my things were easy to identify as valuable or delightful treasures, for example:

- Selected childhood toys, such as some tabletop sports games, toy cars, and model trains.
- Memorabilia from my youth, such as trophies, sports team pictures, and school papers.
- My parents' grandfather clock, the pieces dissembled and in storage in the basement.

- Collections of personal value, such as a road map collection from my childhood and a magazine collection from my young adulthood.
- Most things having to do with my son, such as old toys, artwork, or school projects, even if some of them were broken or in pieces.

The stories these items had to tell were usually compelling, and the scripts that prompted me to keep them made sense to me: *'I loved playing with this electric football game when I was a kid; not ready to give this one away yet ... Oh, this Little League picture is from the year when I made that game-saving catch in center field; gotta keep this one ... I'll definitely want to look through this road map collection again sometime.'*

The process of identifying treasures also highlighted the fact that a lot of my stuff fell into a gray area where deciding what to toss and what to keep wasn't so clear. For example, I found a couple of writing pads that my grandfather would have used when he worked as a conductor on the Pennsylvania Railroad; they were interesting and fun to rediscover, but they weren't treasures, and they weren't meaningful enough to keep either (#76-77; recycled). There were other collections of stuff from my childhood that were also less meaningful to me, but I kept them around for the time being.

There were also gray areas scattered all over the house itself, in particular those places where groups of disparate objects had been gathered together for storage or easy retrieval. I started calling these places "nests," and this preview of a *Scientific American* article about birds' nests (appropriately titled "Treasure in the Trees") helps explain why:

> From twigs and grasses to sheep's wool and horsehair, birds weave their world into their nests. The homes they leave behind thus provide clues about their lives and their environment...

My stashes of stuff were also built with a variety of materials; they provided clues about my life and my environment, and my world was woven into these collections of objects. So the label stuck, and some of my nests could clearly be seen as part of my treasure trove. Several nests contained things that were clearly valuable or useful, such as the coat tree and the recycling area. A few nests were highly organized, such as a closet shelf which held mostly board games and only a few other unrelated items. Some other nests were disorganized, but that didn't bother me if I knew what was in them. Many of these nests could be seen as a source of comfort, a sign of being settled into a home.

Most of my nests, however, were part treasure and part something else. They were mixtures of things organized together for good reasons and things thrown together for no apparent reason, and these nests were not so comforting. Many of them had long ago lost their purpose, such as a broken lock and key (#669, recycled) or never really had one to begin with, such as a red plastic thingy (#666; trashed). Things just gravitated to certain places and settled there without any particular purpose or value. Some nests made it difficult to find things because there were too many other things in the way, especially nests filled with lots of little objects or piles of paper.

Identifying the nests in my house was very helpful for several reasons. Nests were discrete areas, so they were easy to focus on one at a time. Most of them included things that I wanted to remove from my home. Many of them were very visible, so cleaning one up was visually and thus psychologically rewarding. Tackling these nests could also be an unpleasant challenge, however. Most of them contained many objects, so sorting through them involved making lots of individual decisions about what to do with each item. Having too many nests was another problem. There were nests in all the natural nesting places, such as kitchen cabinets, drawers, closets, and shelves. Almost every flat horizontal surface in my home had also reached its nest potential; kitchen countertops, nightstands, the dining room table, the top of my bedroom dresser, and every file cabinet each had a nest of its own.

As a result, my nests exposed the ambiguity of having treasure. Sorting through them revealed how accumulating stuff had expanded my treasure trove to include many items that weren't so treasurable. This complicated the process of determining their purpose and value, and it also reminded me of my prior experience with another treasure trove which had gotten out of hand.

Weakness in Numbers

The expression "strength in numbers" describes how a group can have more influence or power than an individual. This expression accurately describes the power of a group of people, but our possessions often have the opposite effect; accumulating lots of things eventually turns a strength into a weakness.

This is what happened with my parents' stuff. They had spent so much time and energy accumulating and storing so many things because they thought these things would be useful Some Day. Unfortunately, the opposite happened; when Some Day arrived, most of their things were useless. Some of them were broken, such as an old refrigerator and old dryer that they used to store things in the basement. Some had been ruined by mold or rot or other forms of aging. Some had long since lost their purpose, such as unused planners from many years past, blank sheets of graph paper, and more than a thousand VHS movies. Some of them had no clear purpose at all, such as the garbage bins filled with various pieces of metal or the little scraps of wood stored in the old broken dryer even though they were useless for firewood or anything else.

Our parents' house taught us that the converse of the familiar saying, "One's person's trash is another person's treasure," is also true: one person's treasure is another person's trash. Their collections of stuff exemplified weakness in numbers. When Some Day arrived, there were far too many things for us to value them properly, and certainly not in proportion to the way in which they had been carefully collected. The sheer number of things overwhelmed us, and the experience of having to sift through them all made us loathe to keep anything except for a few objects we considered most valuable or precious. As a result, most of our parents' collection of treasures ended up as mounds of trash. Even after salvaging what we could keep or give away or recycle, we ended up filling three-and-a-half freight-sized roll-off containers with their trash. My takeaway from this was simple: *having too many things makes it impossible to value them all.*

Going through the accumulation of our parents' stuff that was in plain sight was daunting enough, but dealing with their buried and hidden treasures was even more challenging.

Buried Treasure

Having buried treasure may sound like a good thing; hearing the phrase might lead you to imagine the prospect of finding a treasure chest full of untold riches that will change your life. Somehow the phrase "buried treasure" makes it easy to forget about how rare it is to find it, how much people suffer in the search for it, or how often what they find is not treasure at all.

Personal treasure troves work the same way, and our parents' home was no exception. Most of the valuable items in their house were buried in an indiscriminate mixture of treasure and junk. Extracting the value of their treasures was more like a salvage operation than a series of delightful discoveries. The only way to reclaim the value of each individual item was to dig it out of a pile, one thing at a time. This made the process of clearing out our parents' house a tedious ordeal. In almost all cases, we had to inspect each item, room by room, drawer by drawer, box by box, and jar by jar. We couldn't just take a bunch of stuff, identify it as trash, and throw it away all at once; we did so at our peril. Once I let my guard down when I found a collection of brown paper bags in their garage. I felt relieved at first to have finally found something I could throw away without having to think about it. But when I started tossing them by the bunches, I soon noticed that some of them seemed just a little bit heavier than the others. I looked inside the bags and to my horror found a credit card, and then another, and another, and still others. When all was said and done, we found over 20 credit cards in these brown paper bags or in bins filled with random objects. Thankfully, all of the credit cards were expired, and none of them had outstanding balances on them, but we didn't know that until we looked at each one.

The bins my father kept on his bedroom floor also embodied the hazards of buried treasure. These bins were filled with random collections of junk intermingled with the occasional keepsake. One especially memorable bin, which I recorded on video for posterity, contained the following items: a hat, a rock, an old pizza coupon, an unused day planner, a plastic bag filled with candy wrappers, and -- oh look, here's my son's birth announcement. These maddening mixtures of valuable and worthless things were everywhere both inside and outside the house. For instance, on top of a trash can in one of the outdoor sheds, my sister found a stack of unopened mail that included an uncashed check for $22,000. Fortunately, the funds were not lost; the check had expired without incident, and the funds had remained in the related account, but there were a few anxious moments until we figured that out.

Burying treasures made it difficult or even impossible to recover their value because it blurred the distinction between treasure and junk. Finding the worthwhile items in random mixtures of stuff often felt like it wasn't worth the effort. At times, we couldn't tell whether our parents were trying to hide their treasures or had simply forgotten about them, and their efforts often seemed out of proportion to the actual value of the items. This was true even when the stuff was worth finding, as when we discovered the treasure that they had hidden all over the house.

Hidden Treasures

We found the first cache of cash in the basement among a random collection of objects in a broken refrigerator, which my dad had "fixed" so that the refrigerator light went on and off when you opened and closed the door, just like a real working refrigerator! Maybe that's why he had resisted my sister's efforts to have it hauled away, even though it had become simply another storage container. The stash was in an old cigar box, which illustrated yet another problem we encountered with our parents' stuff: even the boxes they used to store their stuff might be valuable. These El Producto and Dutch Masters cigar boxes had to be at least 50 years old. Were they worth keeping, or was it better to just throw them away? We were well past caring about cigar boxes by that point, but we were dumbstruck by the monetary treasure stashed inside one of them: rolls and rolls of pennies, categorized and labeled by year, going back to the 1930s.

Soon we found more stashes of pennies in the oddest places. There was a large work cabinet in my dad's basement workroom which he had reclaimed from his own father's basement workroom. There we found several toolboxes, each one filled with more rolls of pennies, also categorized and labeled by year. These discoveries continued in several other random places until we were overcome with amazement and laughter. Our favorite one was the dining room china cabinet, which was the last place we would have thought to look for pennies. Were these stashes of pennies a hidden treasure? Were they trying to hide them on purpose? We'll never know.

Then again, sometimes there is real treasure involved. A colleague of mine told me a story about her husband's grandpa, whose house had big stacks of old newspapers piled up in the hallways and on the bookshelves in the living room. Stacks of newspapers are the epitome of meaningless junk — except when they aren't. In my friend's case, every piece of newspaper had to be carefully examined because in between the papers his family found stock certificates. The monetary value of these certificates stashed among the newspapers was unclear, but it turned out he had also left a notebook in which he had documented all his transactions over a period of many years, and he had died with millions of dollars of diversified investments in his name. (Which made me say about my own parents' stash, "Pennies? Why did it have to be pennies?")

In my own home, a treasure trove of possessions awaited my discovery, even if there were no piles of pennies or stacks of stock certificates stashed among them. There were plenty of things that I had forgotten about, hidden in nests or buried in bins and boxes. Some of these things were treasures; most of them were not. Even so, my relationship with my stuff took another step forward when I treated the process of sorting through my stuff as a treasure hunt. Instead of simply looking for things to toss, I could also look for things to keep. I could change my focus back and forth between "what to keep" and "what to toss," or I could even focus on both at the same time. Having these options gave me a perspective on different ways of relating to my stuff; it was like seeing the task with two eyes instead of one. Identifying my treasures, as well as other items whose value and purpose was clear to me, helped me make healthy distinctions between things that were worth keeping and ones that were not.

At the same time, I also found plenty of places where my things embodied weakness in numbers. Stuff stacked on the basement floor blocked my access to the bins stored on shelves against the wall, so I still didn't know what was in some of them. My home office remained a rather dense collection of nests, or maybe it was just one giant nest. With so many possible nests to choose from, finding candles, flashlights, or duct tape became an irritating chore whenever I couldn't remember the last place I'd put them. It was annoying enough when I couldn't find something I needed; it was even more annoying when I found something in a nest that would have come in handy three months previously if I had known it was there. Even trying to be organized didn't help much sometimes, as when I created folders on particular topics of interest for future reference and then forgot to look at their contents. My things were difficult to value, or lost their value entirely, when they were stored in places where they got in each other's way.

Because my nests were such a common and distinctive form of holding on to my stuff, sorting through them was an effective way to deal with the problem of weakness in numbers. Treating the process of going through a nest as a treasure hunt helped lighten the burden. Identifying an area as a nest also made it easier to choose which stuff to sort through next, for example: *What should I do today? How about going through the nest on that shelf in the living room closet?*

In the process, my nests reminded me how they were more than just storage areas; they were also holding areas, places which enabled me to hold on to my things. By serving as places where my world was indeed woven into the collections of objects that I owned, nests also showed me how holding on to my stuff was a relationship that worked both ways.

Your Turn: Your Treasure Hunt

1) **DIY Treasure Hunt.** Use the list on the next page to do your own treasure hunt:

- *Treasure in Plain Sight* — Identify something that's clearly a treasure to you and is clearly in plain sight. What is it? Where is it?
- *Buried Treasure* — Identify a treasure you found that was "buried" in a nest or some other place. What did you find? Where did you find it?
- *Hidden Treasure* — Identify a treasure you found unexpectedly that was hidden by something else. What did you find? Where was it hiding? How did you feel when you found it?
- Identify another type of treasure that has meaning to you. What is it? Where did you find it? Why is this a treasure to you?

Treasure Type	What You Found	Where You Found It
Treasure in Plain Sight		
Buried Treasure		
Hidden Treasure		
[add your own type]		

2) **Weakness in Numbers.** Identify a place in your house which feels like it has too many things there for you to value them as much as you would like. Where is this place? What kinds of things are there? What can you do about it?

3) **Tackling Your Nests.** Identify a nest in your home. Where is it? What's in it? Then sort through the nest and identify what you find. What things did you find that you want to toss? Did you find any treasures that are worth keeping? Which things are you not sure about? Repeat the process as often as you wish with other nests in your home.

Possession

Another step forward in your relationship with your stuff happens when you understand the power of possession. You might think that possession is about ownership, but it's really more about the individual relationship you have with each and every thing you own, no matter how much or how little you care about that object.

Your relationship with your stuff is a two-way street; you possess your stuff, and it also possesses you. To understand this power of mutual possession, it helped me to consider the many meanings of the words "possess" and "possessed" relative to how my things maintained their hold on me:

- To own: *He possessed a home with many thousands of things inside.*
- To have a particular quality or faculty: *He possessed thoughtfulness and resolve as he sorted through all his stuff.*
- To occupy and control or be occupied and controlled from within: *Sometimes it seemed as if some of his things were possessed by evil spirits.*
- To be spurred or moved by a strong feeling, madness, or a supernatural power; bewitched; under a spell: *Who knows what possessed him to keep that collection for so many years?*
- To keep or maintain a certain state; poised; composed: *Somehow he remained self-possessed most of the time as he sorted through the thousands of things in his basement.*

The common theme in all these definitions was the issue of control. To have a healthier relationship with my stuff, I needed to be in control, and to do that, I needed to understand better how this relationship worked.

Once I started exploring how possessing things was a two-way street, I soon discovered how my reasons for possessing things were the same qualities that enabled them to possess me.

Possessions as Anchors

Sometimes the process of getting rid of a thing was like pulling on a rope that ties an anchor to a boat. The connecting rope is slack, unnoticed and inert until the boat starts to drift too far away, then the rope suddenly tightens with a jolt as the anchor asserts its presence. This was what my things were doing for me, or to me, depending on the situation. They were the anchors that helped keep everything in place; all those stories, mantras, and other inner voices were the ropes, the previously ignored connections between myself and my things which suddenly came into play when I pulled on them.

My possessions anchored me to my home, and making my home an anchorage gave them purpose and value. A home anchored by treasured possessions gave me plenty of benefits: a sense of ease and comfort, a feeling of security or accomplishment or abundance, a source of happiness and joy. Sometimes, though, my house as anchorage felt like a burden that weighed me down and kept my life stuck in place. Larger objects especially made me feel this way because getting rid of them was often difficult, which reminded me that I was still in their possession so long as they were still in mine. This was why it felt really good to get rid of larger things, such as the golf cart (#29), an end table (#673), and the car (#153; all donated). Their departure reduced visual clutter and created more empty space, which helped me feel a little freer and less tied down. Unfortunately, many other large objects remained anchored in place throughout the project. There were plenty of easier things to deal with first, and larger objects were hard to move. What to do with that home gym disassembled in dozens of pieces and stored in the backyard shed? What about that cross-country ski machine which was almost 20 years old? *'That'll be hard for someone to move — maybe best to let that one slide for now.'*

My possessions also anchored my experiences. Connections formed by stories and memories kept many things in place even if they were not treasures. Lots of smaller things had connections that were often surprisingly hard to break. For instance, there was the certificate of appreciation (#104) I'd received for a talk I'd given some years ago. I didn't particularly care about the certificate, and I didn't even remember what the talk was about. But it was a *certificate*. An original. On nice paper stock. *'Surely I could just keep it?'* That rope took a bit of cutting before I eventually recycled the certificate. Then there were the business cards, which collectively represented decades' worth of professional and personal relationships. Even though I'd lost contact with most of these people some time ago, looking at each card evoked a small but fond memory. I had to go through all of the cards individually and remember something about each person before I could cut that rope, let go, and move on (#542-569; recycled).

Time, Energy, and Attention

Henry David Thoreau captured another key quality of possession when he said, "The price of anything is the amount of life you exchange for it." He recognized that money was only one of life's valuable currencies. My possessions also reflected this insight, which explained why their preferred form of exchange was the time, energy, and attention they demanded from me.

In many cases, of course, I paid this price willingly. After all, that was the main reason for owning things: to use them, enjoy them, and benefit from having them. Whenever my stuff fulfilled these purposes, their demands on my time, energy, and attention were agreeable, and the transaction costs hardly ever even crossed my mind. As Thoreau also recognized, however, this transaction applied to all one's stuff, and mine was no different. I incurred the costs of possession whenever I engaged with my things, whether I wanted to or not.

My old car was a perfect example of this. I'd bought it new, kept it for more than 13 years, and put more than 200,000 miles on it. I felt that I'd gotten my money's worth in terms of what's commonly called Total Cost of Ownership (purchase price plus operational costs), but the actual cost to me of owning that car — call it the Truly Total Cost of Ownership — was far greater when the time, energy, and attention costs were included. Filling the car with gas, washing the exterior, cleaning up the latest spill on the upholstery, searching for the keys when I misplaced them, trying to find the most recent registration and insurance card in the overstuffed glove compartment — you get the idea. Getting the car repaired was an especially large time, energy, and attention expense: listening to strange noises the car made and wondering whether it was time for another repair appointment, spending time deciding to put off the repair appointment, finally making the repair appointment, moving other appointments around to accommodate the repair appointment, driving to the repair shop, arranging alternative transportation, waiting at the repair shop for the car to be ready, worrying about whether the repairs would be done properly and on time, making sure the bill was accurate, and so on.

It was easy to overlook these costs when buying something because I had learned to make such decisions in terms of purchase price while ignoring the other costs of ownership, whether these costs were large or small. For instance, purchase price was a factor when deciding which dress shirts to buy, but including the monetary cost of owning them, such as laundering, dry cleaning, or electricity use, never occurred to me. Starting to notice these monetary costs helped me understand better how mutual possession formed; spending more money on things I already owned increased my valuation of them, which in turn increased their hold on me.

It was even more revealing to notice the added time, energy, and attention costs of my dress shirts, such as ironing, cleaning stains, deciding which one to wear, or recalling places and experiences from previous times I wore one of them. Collectively, these costs could be called the Total Cost of Relationship, as they reflected how my relationship with these shirts was a function of spending time, energy, and attention on them, as was the mutual possession which formed as a result. This explained why I needed to recall a few moments in my relationship with a couple of these dress shirts before donating them (#775-776).

Looking at my stuff through the lens of mutual possession made me notice the alarming amount of time, energy, and attention my things required. It was almost as if they were zombies, silently and patiently waiting for a moment of my attention to awaken them. Even seemingly innocuous objects were *time sinks, energy drains,* and *attention wasters-in-waiting*, ready to engage with me on cue and demand their due.

It was even scarier to discover that my things demanded my time, energy, and attention simply by being there. They were draining energy from my life without my being aware of it. This claim on my time, energy, and attention reminded me of a more bewitching creature: vampires.

Possessions as Vampires

Calling possessions "vampires" may sound far fetched, but in fact vampires of another sort already occupied my home. They were called "energy vampires," one of the names used to describe the many appliances and devices plugged in to outlets in almost every home, consuming energy even when not in use. Also called "vampire devices" or "phantom load," these vampires drain a lot more power than one might think; the Lawrence Berkeley National Laboratory estimates that vampire devices account for almost 10 percent of residential electricity use. Unless one unplugs every single device when not in use, this power drainage happens all the time, simply by being there.

Dealing with my stuff drew power from my life in a number of ways, whether it was moving things around, putting things away, organizing things, cleaning up for the cleaning ladies, or something else. Even just having to look for things could drain a lot of time, energy, and attention, especially when there were a lot of them. As my brother-in-law put it, "When you have a lot of things, you spend a lot of time looking for things." He estimated that he had spent at least 20 percent of his waking time looking for things in the house they had lived in for 30 years. (After moving to a new home, he upped his estimate to 25 percent.) Even a much smaller "phantom load" of, say, six percent equates to about an hour per day. Add in the energy and attention demands, and clearly I was exchanging a considerable chunk of my life as the price of possession.

Not all of my possessions demanded my time, energy, and attention. I owned many things that had remained unplugged from my life, things that I hadn't engaged with or even thought about for years. These things demanded nothing of me so long as I ignored them, but paying attention to them changed the dynamic, as if I'd plugged them in and turned on the power. Even small or seemingly trivial things exerted this power, such as a Raggedy Ann doll, a music box, and a candlestick holder (#675-677; all donated). Being thoughtful about their fate only upped the amperage; recalling the stories, listening to the inner voices, and making thoughtful decisions all required more time, energy, and attention than if I had been thoughtless about the process. Almost every single item I encountered went from asking nothing to asking something once I paid attention to it, and in some cases that something was a lot more than I expected or wanted.

The Bassinet Story

The bassinet (#672) was probably the biggest example of an object that took much longer to get rid of than I'd ever intended. I didn't want it; I had no use for it; I didn't really like it, and I didn't care about it. So how did it extract so much time, energy, and attention from me?

The bassinet was made of wood and had foldable legs with wheels on them, so you could carry the bassinet like a large basket or extend the legs to waist height and roll it around a room. It seemed pretty old to me, although I didn't know how old. We must have used it for our newborn son at least for a short time, although I couldn't remember doing so. It must have been in decent condition when we'd first gotten it, but it no longer looked very usable. The bedding was in need of washing and mending, and the frame possibly needed a paint job as well.

At first I thought about simply throwing it out, but I remembered that we'd paid money for it, although I don't know how much. That and its apparent age made me think, 'It might be worth something; I can't just throw it out. We (may have) paid a lot for that; I can't just give it away.' So I tried putting it on Craigslist a couple of times, but there was not even a nibble. A couple of Freecycle listings found no takers either. Then I went to a small shop nearby that sold vintage collectibles to see if they'd be interested. The owner said that we could possibly work out a consignment deal if there was interest; perhaps I could bring it to her shop that coming Saturday to display outside on the sidewalk? Now this was really getting ridiculous; give up the good part of a Saturday for an object I didn't care about, just to see if someone might be interested in buying it? This did not appeal to me, so I didn't follow up on the offer.

Having sunk so much time into this bassinet, I decided to try selling it one more time. I took a couple of pictures of it, along with several other objects which fell into the same general category of Being Old Enough to Be Worth Something Possibly, and went to the Antiques Row district in a nearby town. One by one I went to several shops, showed the proprietors the pictures, and got a series of polite no's, sometimes tinged with that beyond disinterested, uniquely disdainful 'what-kind-of-place-do-you-think-I-run-here?' response that antique shop owners can do so well. Finally I discovered a shop that was actually an antique charity thrift store; when I showed them the pictures, they said they would take all of my things. I promptly went back to my house, loaded up the car, returned to the store, and dropped off everything there, including the bassinet, an end table, an old suitcase, and the Raggedy Ann doll, music box, and candlestick holder (#672-677).

My experience with the bassinet made me feel that the process of determining how much time, energy, and attention my things received was not entirely in my control. It even felt at times as if the process was being guided by forces larger than myself, as if my possessions had put me under some sort of spell. This may sound overly dramatic, but it didn't feel that way to me. After all, this wasn't the first time that I'd fallen under the spell of things.

Possessed by Ornaments

My parents' grandfather clock was not the only thing from their house that ended up in mine. Among my treasures were several boxes of toy cars, a green slot car, and enough HO model train cars to make a small five-car train with engine and caboose. I'd kept these mementos because looking at them instantly brought back fond childhood memories of Christmas holiday seasons. At the center of these festivities was the Christmas platform display in the living room, filled with objects which now evoked vivid memories. There was the Plasticville village with its tiny houses and fire station and ice cream drive-in stand, along with the HO train and Model Motoring cars zooming around on their tracks under the tree. In the evenings, we turned on a color wheel light that made the tree turn red, blue, amber, and green as we sat contentedly in the living room watching or taking part in the platform proceedings.

My collection of childhood holiday mementos also included a number of Christmas ornaments which had once adorned many a brightly decorated tree as the centerpiece of our family's holiday platform displays. These ornaments were part of an extensive collection of Christmas decorations my parents had kept. Most of the ornaments in their collection were familiar from our childhoods, but we also discovered unfamiliar ones that must have belonged to our grandparents. There were icicle-shaped ornaments and birds with rusty metal clips and ones shaped like bunches of fruit and ones painted with old style clocks. Some of them were likely 100 years old or more but far from mint condition, well-worn from many years of use.

The fate of these ornaments became a family story for the ages. Here is my version of the story, which I call *Possessed by Ornaments*. We three siblings decided to keep the ornaments, but we couldn't agree on an easy way to figure out who got which ones, so we settled on taking turns. Sitting on the carpet of our parents' living room, we divided up box after box of ornaments, choosing them in turn. One. By. One. Prized groups of ornaments like the birds and the icicles were divided equally among the three of us rather than keeping them together as sets. It could have made more sense to divvy up entire boxes of ornaments of the same color by box — 'Why don't you take this box of red/silver/blue ones and I'll take that one' — but we divided up those ornaments one at a time instead.

Meanwhile, the other family members watched with looks of silent horror on their faces. I imagined them thinking thoughts like, *They've gone crazy. These are the elders of our family now? This family is in deep trouble.* They watched us spend at least two or three hours going through a couple thousand or so ornaments in this way, and to this day, I cannot really explain what possessed us to do this. Some odd combination of attachments and perceived fairness was involved, but there was more to it than that. Let's just call it the power of possession.

Holding on and Letting Go

None of my possessions put me under a similar spell during my project, but there were many signs of lingering attachments. There were objects like the bassinet which took much longer to get rid of than I wanted. Many of my things exerted a vampire effect, extracting my time, energy, and attention whether I was aware of it or not.

Fortunately, the project also created a reverse vampire effect. Letting go of things, unplugging them from my life, and having fewer things to engage with enabled me to regain more of my time, energy, and attention.

Getting rid of hundreds of things released their hold on me, creating more psychological and emotional space as new physical spaces opened up in my house as well.

Discovering the power of possession as relationship was another important step forward on my journey. Possessing stuff was mutual; we owned each other. Getting rid of things thoughtfully awakened their power to possess, tugging back at me when I tried to pull them away. The anchoring power of possessions was fine for the things I wanted to keep, but not when it kept me from moving on physically or emotionally in my life. Possession was also a two-way transaction; the benefits I received from having my things came at the cost of the time, energy, and attention they demanded from me. Keeping these demands in balance and under control was one of the keys to building a healthy relationship with my stuff.

The project was teaching me a lot about my ways of holding on to stuff. Each of my things had a story to tell. Inner voices ran constantly in the background of my mind making decisions about what to do with my things, mostly by telling me why I should keep them. The process of sorting through my possessions with thoughtful attention reminded me why some of my things were treasures but also showed me how accumulating stuff was often an unhealthy way of holding on to it. Having learned so much about holding on to my stuff, it was now time to learn more about how to let it go.

❈❈❈❈❈❈❈❈❈❈❈❈❈

Your Turn: Your Relationship with Your Possessions

1) **Possessions as Anchors.** Identify one or more of your possessions that anchor your life. For each possession, label whether that possession keeps you in place in a healthy or unhealthy way, then:

- For each "healthy" anchor, list the benefits it provides: ease and comfort? A feeling of security or accomplishment or abundance? A source of happiness and joy? Connection with a fond memory or past experience? Something else?
- For each "unhealthy" anchor, describe how that possession feels unhealthy to you. Do it make you feel weighed down or as if your life is stuck in place? Is it a burden in some other way? What do you wish to do with that possession, and how will you act on that wish?

Healthy Possessions:	Benefit(s) It Provides	
1)		
2)		
3)		
Unhealthy Possessions:	How It Feels Unhealthy	What You Will Do with It
1)		
2)		
3)		

2) **Time, Energy, and Attention.** Reflect on how one or more of your possessions demands your time, energy, and attention (TEA):

- How does each one demand more TEA than you may have realized?
- How much of this extra TEA feels like it's worthwhile? How much of it feels like a waste?
- How does this reflection change your perception of this possession?

Part III: Letting Go

Curation

Things, you've got to let me know
Should I keep or let you go?
If I say that you are mine
You'll be here until I die
So I got to let you know
Should I keep or let you go?
[with apologies to The Clash]

Letting go of your stuff is also about more than just getting rid of it. Simple disposal will work with a few items, but most of your belongings have stronger attachments, and they will resist your efforts if you try to simply get rid of them. As I learned during my project, you can overcome this resistance by learning how to transfer the power of deciding what to do with your stuff from your things to yourself, and you can develop several useful skills for doing this:

- Focusing on how you hold on to your things by listening to their stories, attending to your internal dialogue, and managing their possessive demands can help loosen their hold on you.
- Focusing on what to keep by identifying your treasures and other valued objects can make it easier to let other, less valued items go.
- Learning how to choose whether to focus on what to keep (holding on), what to toss (letting go), or on both at the same time, will help you make healthier distinctions between what's worth keeping and what's not.

Each of these skills can help you be in charge of the decision-making process, but you will eventually find that using them is not always enough. In my case, shifting the focus of my project from holding on to things to learning how to let go of them prompted me to hear a tune in my brain with lyrics something like the ones above. This tune sang loudly about the tension between keeping something and letting it go, and it played in my head for a few reasons. Tackling more nests meant having more decisions to make about what to keep and what to let go. Making progress through the project had a curious downside: the more things I got rid of, the more difficult the process became. Most of the relatively easy stuff was gone, and far fewer of the remaining things offered easy decisions about what to do with them. Also, more of the things I encountered were part of larger collections, and dealing with these revealed a few new varieties of holding on to stuff. As a result, I needed to find some new strategies for sorting through my collections before I could sing all of the words in this new tune.

Collecting

The Smithsonian is the largest museum and research complex in the world, with 19 museums and galleries, nine research facilities, and a zoo (the National Zoological Park in Washington, DC). Visitors to the Smithsonian's museums are routinely impressed by the sheer volume and scale of the displays; there are over a million objects in building after huge building covering over 2.7 million square feet of display area. One photograph alone (a 3,375 square foot pinhole photo of an airplane hangar) covers more square footage than my entire house.

Massive as they are, these displays are not even the tip of the iceberg; less than two percent of the 155 million objects in the entire Smithsonian collection is on view at any one time. The vast bulk of the collection is housed behind the scenes in the museums themselves, in other off-site storage facilities, and at the Smithsonian's state-of-the-art Museum Support Center in Suitland, Maryland. Think of the closing scene in the movie *Raiders of the Lost Ark*, in which the ark was put into a nondescript wooden crate and stored in a gigantic warehouse, to be lost and forgotten among the endless rows of other identical wooden crates. Now think much, much bigger than that, because the actual Smithsonian storage facilities are far larger than what is depicted in the movie.

The mind-boggling scale of this collection is why the Smithsonian is sometimes affectionately referred to as "America's attic." Although the main purpose of the Smithsonian collection is to foster "the increase and diffusion of knowledge," the museum's role in amassing and storing valuable objects resonates more with most Americans because this relationship also works in reverse. If the Smithsonian is "America's attic," then America's attics, along with its basements and garages and spare rooms and sheds and barns, are small-scale museums commemorating individual households, families, and their lives. Millions of us have our own personal Smithsonians, and my house was certainly no exception.

My Personal Smithsonian

There was no shortage of collections in my personal Smithsonian: household furnishings, recreational equipment, gardening tools, childhood games, and boxes of photographs, just to name a very few. Some of these were designated as personal treasures, while others had accumulated for no apparent reason. Once I became aware of this process, however, I owned up to it. Things didn't just accumulate; I collected them — collected them and held on to them.

One of my largest collections was an accumulation of office papers. I had several filing cabinets, about a dozen bins, and a few shelves full of paper. Like a lot of people, I kept paper copies of bank statements, utility bills, mortgage documents and tax returns. I also kept paper copies of work related to my consulting business, such as documents produced for clients, meeting notes, and documents my clients had given me. It wasn't that I felt a need to hold onto every single piece of paper. I recycled plenty of shredded and other paper documents, for instance some old invoices (#947), prospectuses (#777-782), and various work-related print publications (#586; #783; #929-931). Others had been scanned and put into digital folders first before recycling them (for example, #124-128; #131-151; #952-961).

Still, I usually felt some resistance whenever I got rid of paper files and documents, and I heard some new inner voices in the process. *'There could be valuable work in there. I put a lot of thought and effort into creating those documents. Maybe I could use them on a future project. Better keep them just in case I need them again someday.'* These documents were the products of more than a decade's worth of work in a successful business; many of them contained original ideas, insights, and other potentially useful creations. Often I kept paper copies even if I also had a digital copy or two somewhere. *'It feels more immediate and useful somehow in paper form.'*

Despite what these inner voices were saying, in reality I had no idea what was valuable in there. It dawned on me that saving office files was an old habit guided by a larger, simple mantra: Keep Paper Files for as long as possible. This mantra made sense to me since so many of my belongings were made of paper, and it was still useful to keep some paper documents. Even so, the result was another case of weakness in numbers; it was hard to find things in my office because there were so many paper files stored in filing cabinets and bins on the floor. I knew which old projects were in a particular bin or filing cabinet, but I couldn't really tell what was in each folder so finding a particular document or work product was definitely not easy.

There was also another, stranger idea at work, a lingering notion that I was preserving history, as if someone in the future might want to look through my things as a form of cultural anthropology. I could imagine this someone sifting through the artifacts of a typical home office from the late twentieth/early twenty-first century. *'Look, here's a document that was clearly printed on an Apple IIe, circa 1987, during the dot matrix printer period. Now, this one here is clearly more recent; this font was not widely used until the mid-1990s...'* Digging deeper into my paper collections, this imaginary anthropologist might also be delighted to find a historical record of the transition between a paper-based and a digital-based enterprise, as evidenced by the old exam books written in ink and the typewritten papers from college with some of the white outs and typeovers still visible. All thanks to My Personal Smithsonian.

This notion was not entirely strange; after all, we all grapple with the issue of how to manage our personal legacy, but it was worth asking myself where this notion came from in the first place. Why was it my responsibility to be the keeper of this history? Surely there were still millions of these things out there. Why should I be the one to hold onto them in my own personal museum? The answer, I realized, described another, more problematic way of holding on to things.

Grasping

Grasping was the act of collecting and holding on to things for a variety of reasons, or for no particular reason at all. It was another form of mutual possession; as my possessions held on to me, I grasped them right back. Grasping often felt like my first impulse whenever I encountered a new object; the object's story presented itself, the inner voices started talking, and my grasping reflex kicked in and held on unless I found an overriding reason for letting go. This helped explain why I had so much stuff: when grasping was a default setting and when there was no override, accumulating things was the inevitable result.

The urge to grasp is strong, and the 1,000 Things Project did not remove that urge from me. One of the driving forces behind this urge was a mantra which I called Preserving Memories. For instance, I donated an old suitcase (#674) to charity because I knew I was never going to use it again. Some weeks later, I looked at the picture I had taken of the suitcase and noticed the initials "A.G.S." on it. A sudden stab of regret hit me: oh no, maybe I should have kept it as a piece of family history. What would my family say? Um, wait a second. Who in my family even had these initials? It turned out that these initials were my grandmother's first, maiden, and married name, and a family member reassured me that my decision to donate the suitcase was fine. This made me wonder why I'd felt any regret at all. The suitcase itself was not a family heirloom, and it made no sense to hold on to it as a bit of family history because whatever stories or memories the suitcase had held were already lost to us. This meant that the suitcase was no different from any other object which was lost or long forgotten or never even known about.

I also had collections of things for which I had forgotten the stories, for instance mementos from former students who had given them to me as tokens of gratitude. They reminded me of treasures we'd found in our parents' attic when clearing out their house. A particularly memorable find was two 10-inch tall German bibles from the eighteenth century. Although these objects were fascinating in their own right, their value as family heirlooms was diminished because we didn't know the history or the stories behind them. We had never asked about their history because we'd never even known they existed. This illustrates another danger of grasping too many things: forgetting their stories or failing to pass their stories on to others diminishes their meaning.

While I felt sad that I couldn't remember the story or sometimes even the person behind some of the things I'd collected, I usually held on to them anyway in case I remembered sometime in the future. The urge to grasp is strong, after all. Every so often, though, this urge gave way to an even stronger force: the urge to purge.

Purging

Purging can refer to a healthy process. It's the urge that drives countless spring cleanings. It's the relief of seeing a cleaned-out closet or the satisfaction of clearing out a corner of a basement. It's the calm that comes from reducing the vampire load of things as they disappear from thought and even memory after they've been physically removed. Purging was great when it felt like that.

Unfortunately, purging can also be the result of feeling overwhelmed, stressed out, or out of patience, when "Enough already!" becomes an outburst of thoughtlessly throwing stuff away. This form of purging was not so great, and my project had its moments of thoughtless purging now and then. Sometimes it resulted from cleaning out a nest which involved sorting through too many small objects. After a while, my patience wore out, and things would start going in the trash without much thought, such as a collection of miscellaneous office junk (#715-726) along with some "assorted small items from [a] bag" (#728-747). Other times, an individual item exhausted my patience, such as a red plastic stadium horn (#588; recycled), an old roll of film that I would never develop (#859; trashed), or a tape measure that didn't work very well (#941; trashed). The process of trying to figure out a better fate for each of these items overwhelmed me; decision fatigue set in, and I finally just said, "The hell with it" and tossed them in the recycling or trash. More often, I deferred the decision by reverting to grasping — holding on to the thing even if I really couldn't tell you why.

My parents' house was much worse; the sheer number and volume of individual items there overwhelmed our ability to value them, which often pushed my family members and myself into this "Enough already!" purging mode. During such moments, we would throw away everything we encountered except for a few things we considered most valuable or precious. Even then, there were moments of hesitation where one of us would identify a random thing — I specifically remember a Mickey Mouse watch and a vacuum cleaner attachment -- and we would say out loud, 'This could be useful; maybe we should keep this.' In response, everyone else would look at that person and start laughing until he or she came to his or her senses, remembered the reality of the situation, and tossed the thing into the dumpster.

The Color Chest Story

The strange collections of things that filled our parents' house also triggered our urge to purge. Some of these collections were strange because they consisted of random objects, such as the ones in the bins my father kept in his bedroom. Other collections were even stranger because they were clearly organized but with no apparent purpose, such as the barrels of scrap wood and window parts, the jars of fasteners and electrical supplies, and the metal coffee cans filled with all sorts of small items.

An old bedroom dresser in the basement held an especially strange collection of objects whose purpose was mystifying even though its organizing principle was clear. This otherwise nondescript chest was painted gray, but we started calling it the color chest after discovering what was inside its drawers. Each one was filled with old toys and other small objects, all sorted by color. There was a drawer filled with nothing but red toys and other assorted red objects. Another drawer was filled with blue toys and objects; one was filled with pink ones, one with yellow ones, one with green ones, and one with black ones. Other than having a common color, none of the objects in each drawer related to any of the other objects in that drawer except by chance, for instance two plastic cars or toy dinosaurs from the same set that happened to be the same color. Some of the objects were broken or had missing pieces; a few of them had no discernible purpose at all. We could not help but laugh and shake our heads in wonder as we disposed of the color chest and other collections as best we could by recycling the metal coffee cans and fasteners, salvaging a few of the toys as keepsakes, and tossing out much of the rest.

My own possessions did not include anything quite so strange as the color chest, but some of my collections made me feel a little uneasy and led me to question their purpose. What was the point of keeping all those gardening supplies in the shed if I never did any gardening? Why have a collection of board games if no one ever played them? What about all those drawers filled with random combinations of things? Perhaps internal mantras like Preserving Memories and My Personal Smithsonian were symptoms of a more serious ailment. Collecting, purging, and organizing could be useful, but when collecting became grasping, or when purging was a reaction to being overwhelmed, or when organizing served no rational purpose, then they became toxic — if not a disease, then certainly a dis-ease. The Lonely Planet guide describes the Smithsonian Institution as America's attic "if America was a quirky grandfather." At times, my own collections of things made me feel as if I too was on the way to becoming a quirky grandfather, or worse. Fortunately, even if my Smithsonianesque tendencies made me feel ill at ease, the Smithsonian and its fellow museums also offered a way to a cure.

The Curative Powers of Curation

Museums collect with a purpose. They amass collections, but they also *curate* them. They are highly selective about the objects they take; even the Smithsonian's vast collection represents only a tiny fraction of the donations that are offered to them. Museums are also very careful about taking care of the objects they keep. My project was nowhere near as involved as curating a museum collection, but the practice of curation appealed to me because it fit well with my project goals. Like a museum curator, I had responsibility for a collection of objects; my job was to oversee their care, and I was also in charge of figuring out their purpose and value.

The practice of curation as a way of building a healthier relationship with my stuff was also appealing. Could curating my things be a cure for the mindless grasping, purging, and organizing which too often afflicted my relationship with my stuff? After all, the words cure, curative, and curation are all derived from words with interrelated meanings: to cure, take care of, pay attention, manage, heal. These all described healthy ways of relating to my things: managing them, taking care of them, and paying attention to them (but not too much attention!) while curing myself from the need to hold on to them in unhealthy ways.

This inspired me to adapt the practice of curation to my personal collection of stuff. The most relevant elements of applying a museum-style approach to curating things were selection, value, storage, and display. I focused mainly on selection and value during the project, which enabled me to find effective strategies for letting go of my stuff.

Curation Strategies

The first and most common type of strategy I found was *culling*. Cultivating the art of culling was a great response to the My Personal Smithsonian mantra because it shifted the focus of collecting stuff from *amassing* it to *selecting* it. Learning how to cull was especially helpful for dealing with collections because it enabled me to make decisions about my things *relative to each other* rather than deciding what to do with each object individually.

The most basic definition of culling is to select, pick, or choose, and the first stage in the culling process often involved a strategy I'd already been using throughout the project. **Starting with the easy stuff** was how I launched the project; the first 70 items I got rid of were ones that had been identified for removal before the project began. Many of my nests contained a few easy targets to start with, and items that were clearly trash also fell into this category. This strategy was also useful for picking out the first one or two items to remove from some of my other collections. Over the course of the project, though, the easy pickings tapered off as I got rid of more things, and this strategy became harder to use. It also didn't work very well with most collections because they were composed of items with roughly equal value; there was no "easy" stuff to cull.

Culling a collection required finding ways to choose which items to get rid of. Once again, I found it helpful to consider the meanings of the word, which reminded me of the expression "culling the herd." This idiom encompasses several different methods of culling, such as removing weaker or undesirable members, reducing a herd to a manageable size, or exterminating the herd entirely. My collections were definitely herd-like, and each of these methods related to picking something out for a reason. As a result, their subtle differences in meaning helped me find several distinct strategies to use in different situations, depending on a collection's contents:

Thinning out the herd — This strategy involved reducing the number of things to a manageable size and was especially useful for dealing with nests. Very few nests disappeared entirely since most of them contained a few items that were worth keeping, but some nests got considerably smaller and much more manageable after being culled. For example, I thinned out my collection of CDs by removing outdated software programs, ones with scratches or other damage, and other "weaker or undesirable members" of that herd (#804-853; trashed). Yearly visits to the eye doctor had resulted in a much larger collection of contact lens cases than I could possibly use, so I kept two of them and recycled the rest (#990-999).

A variation of this thinning out strategy was to keep most of the items in a collection and only let go of a few. This worked well for collections which had no easy items, such as clothes that were still wearable. Usually I only wanted to part with a few pieces of clothing at any one time, so I selected items to give away that meant less to me relative to the others. I also thinned out my book collection by a few dozen or so through donations (e.g., #909-923), gifts (#95, 786-798), or recycling ones that were clearly outdated or no longer useful (#98, 854-856, 928-931, 951).

Exterminating the herd — This strategy involved getting rid of a collection completely, for example my collections of conference tote bags, conference lanyards, license plates, and used printer cartridges. Sometimes I did this all at once, as with the license plates, while other times I did this over time, as with the conference tote bags and lanyards.

Picking representatives — This strategy involved sorting through my collections, picking out a representative sample of things from the ones that I valued, and letting the other ones go. For instance, I used this strategy with my collection of business cards (#542-569) by recycling most of them, but I kept a few as reminders of my past work life. I also used this strategy with a collection of old T-shirts, keeping some of them to represent a few of my life stories and then letting go of the remainder (#757-764; donated).

There was a variation of this strategy that I called *idea mining.* My bins full of folders became idea mines, places where I could find original ideas, insights, and other valuable nuggets from my work products, extract them from the rest of the documents put them in a special folder, and rid of the rest of the documents. I used this strategy extensively to cull my massive collections of papers (e.g., #971-75, #980-82; recycled) in a way that made sense to me. The notion of extracting was key because it enabled me to treat the rest of the stuff as leftover material, which could be disposed of responsibly without losing anything of value. Idea mining helped me let go of a lot of accumulated paper without regrets.

Since my project focused on letting go of stuff, storage and display strategies were less important to me, but there were a few exceptions. Collections of identified keepsakes were put into a few designated storage areas. I also started storing some items more visibly on open shelving, in clear or translucent bins, or in open nests to remind myself that I would have to deal with them again sooner or later even if I wasn't quite ready to do so at the moment. I also became aware that my home contained several display nests, including the family pictures on top of the piano, the cluster of mementos on my bedroom dresser, and the array of bowls, vases, and other beautiful objects on my dining room table. While sorting through a nest, occasionally I would find some valued object and decide to take it out and put it on display.

Not all of my curation strategies worked as well as I would have liked. For instance, I set up a couple of "staging nests" to store things that were ready for removal. One of the staging nests was near the front door to serve as a constant visual reminder to get rid of the stuff sooner rather than later. Instead, the stuff just sat there for months at a time, and I got used to neglecting it. The other staging nest was on a table underneath the basement steps, and it was even easier to ignore because it was out of my sight most of the time. Staging nests helped remind me what things should go but not with deciding where they should go, so they didn't help speed up the process, and they didn't help with doing the process thoughtfully either.

Overall, though, curation was a powerful practice for letting go of things, and the curative powers of curation helped me build a healthier relationship with my stuff. Making decisions about my things relative to each other by cultivating the art of culling helped me to identify the purpose or value of my things more clearly. Culling my collections made it easier to appreciate the items I kept while letting go of others without regret. Culling strategies gave me lots of options, but they weren't always strong enough to overcome My Personal Smithsonian tendencies or address my need for Preserving Memories. Letting go of things in these cases required me to find a different set of strategies that worked by turning the power of attachment to my advantage.

❋ ❋ ❋ ❋ ❋ ❋ ❋ ❋ ❋ ❋ ❋ ❋ ❋

Your Turn: Your Curation Experiences

1) **Your "Personal Smithsonian."** Which of your belongings most make you feel as if you have your own personal Smithsonian collection in your house? Which of these items are on display in your home? Which of them are in storage, and why? Which of them are you holding on to as part of your personal, familial or historical legacy?

2) **Your Experience with Purging.**
    - Recall an instance where you did some "healthy" purging. What kind of purge was it? (Spring cleaning, closet cleaning, garage cleaning, etc.) How did it make you feel? (Name one or more of the emotions.)
    - Recall an instance where you did some "unhealthy" purging. Name one or more feelings or states of mind which triggered it

(overwhelmed, stressed out, out of patience, something else). How did you feel afterwards?
- Name one action you could take to assure that your next purge feels more like a healthy one.

3) **Your Curation Strategies.** Use the table below to identify which curation strategies you have used for sorting through your stuff. For each strategy, identify what collection(s) or other specific items you used this for, and briefly describe how it worked or didn't work for you. Did it feel curative, healing, or otherwise healthy for you? If so, how or why?

Curation Strategy	What Collection(s)/Item(s) You Used This For	How It Worked/ Didn't Work
Thinning Out the Herd [or your name for this]		
Exterminating the Herd [or your name for this]		
Picking Representatives [or your name for this]		
Idea Mining		
[add your own strategy(ies) here]		

Gratitude

Connecting with the power of gratitude is another great way of letting things go.

Gratitude works a little differently from other ways of letting go. Listening to stories, attending to internal dialogue, managing the demands of possession, and identifying your treasures all lead to *disconnecting* the power of your attachment to individual items. Using various culling strategies helps you disconnect attachments by comparing the value of your things relative to one another. By comparison, gratitude actually *uses* the power of attachment to help you let things go. Here's how it worked for me:

- My house still held a lot of stuff that I didn't want, need, or use.
- Someone else might want or need or use some of this stuff.
- Other people would be happy, even *grateful* to have stuff I gave away.
- The things that drained my energy could actually give other people energy if they owned them.
- In this way, I could *use* the power of attachment to help me let things go instead of just relying on disconnecting my attachments to them.

This insight transformed my unwanted, unneeded, and unused stuff into a potential power source. Instead of being a burden or a future pile of junk, *my things were a valuable resource for generating gratitude*. These largely untapped reserves were hidden in plain sight, just waiting for me to extract and release them. I was sitting on a gold mine of good will, a reservoir of positive energy to give to the world, and there were several ways of using the power of attachment to generate gratitude.

The Gratitude of Giving Things Away

Giving things away might seem like an obvious way to generate gratitude, but to be honest, it wasn't exactly automatic for me. My inner voices often expressed very different opinions about what to do with certain things: *'I might use that again someday.'* *'It's probably worth something. I should get some money for it.'* The more valuable the object, the harder it often was to let it go. Besides, while I was vaguely aware that people might be grateful for the things they received from me, generating gratitude by giving stuff away was not a focus of my project at first. I didn't expect anything more than a simple "thank you" now and then, so it surprised me a bit when people took the time to express a few words of appreciation or to tell me how they would use the thing and why they were grateful to have it. It surprised me even more when I started feeling gratified about giving things away. Of course, feeling good about giving to others is timelessly human and nothing new, but it took me a while to fully appreciate the power of mutual gratitude — how giving things away could generate gratitude in myself as well as others.

The act of giving things away generated gratitude by releasing the power and energy of my stuff to make new connections in the world. The recipients of my things formed their own attachments to them while creating new stories in the process. For instance, after I gave away an old golf push cart (#29; Freecycled) early in the project, the recipient sent me this email message:

> Thanks so much. Just last weekend I played golf with my son and I was telling him that if I'm going to start using a cart, I need to get one rather than rent it. This is just what I was thinking of.

I hadn't expected to learn anything more about the golf cart once it was gone, but it was gratifying to find out that giving it away enabled a father and son to spend time together, so reading this story created mutual gratitude.

Sometimes, the process of giving something away was a story in itself, as was the case with a plastic toy storage bin (#600). It took me a long time to find a new home for this bin, mainly because I resisted letting it go. The bin was durable and weather-resistant (*'See? It's useful! Maybe I need to keep it...'*), so it spent a long time outside on the front porch holding various toys until I consolidated them into another bin. Even though the bin was no longer needed, I kept it anyway, thinking that *'maybe my niece and her family could use it for some of their young daughter's toys. Best keep it on the porch Just in Case.'* Eventually it dawned on me that transporting an old, somewhat dirty bin 150 miles might not be preferable to buying a new, clean toy bin at a nearby store instead. One by one, the inner voices fell away until I finally got the gumption to put the storage bin on Freecycle, where my offer was quickly taken by someone who wanted to use the bin for storing garden tools and supplies outside. We arranged a time for pickup, and I put it on my front porch. A couple came over to pick it up while I happened to be home. I hadn't planned to go out and greet them until I noticed that they seemed to be there longer than I expected. I went out to see what was going on and discovered that they were having problems putting the bin into their mid-size car, so I tried to help. The bin was too big for the trunk, and it would not squeeze into the back seat either. They were clearly looking forward to having the bin, but they were about ready to give up. Finally I noticed that the bin would fit fine in the back of my car and asked them how far away they lived. When they said about 20 minutes away, I offered to put the bin in my car and drive it over to their house for them. After some initial hesitation, they agreed, so I followed them over to their house, unloaded the bin, received their thanks, and returned home.

This was a lot of time to spend on giving something away; some might even say it was a waste of time. But from the perspective of generating mutual gratitude, it was well worth it. Recipients of my stuff were often so clearly grateful, and the experience made me realize that giving things away was far more satisfying then any money I would have received from selling them.

My stuff didn't have to be large in size or monetary value to generate mutual gratitude. Friends and relatives gratefully received some children's books (#786-798), a cookie tin returned to its owner (#857), and a bundle of knitting stuff (#939), which made me feel grateful that these things had found good homes. I even created mutual gratitude by giving away a cardboard box, some foam pieces, and some bubble wrap (#468-471). I'd used them to bring some presentation materials to a conference workshop and then encountered a colleague who was trying to figure out how to ship home some bottles of wine she had bought. My packing materials worked perfectly for her purpose, and it saved me the trouble of taking them all home.

The Gratitude of Revisiting and Preserving Memories

Despite the difficulties of clearing out my parents' house, engaging in the process of dealing with their stuff generated other types of gratitude on many occasions. There were moments of appreciation for the excuse to spend time together with family members working on a common task. There was the simple gratitude that came from making progress on the work at hand, and there was the mutual gratitude that we felt for everyone's efforts to get the job done.

Engaging with the stuff itself was another source of gratitude. Discovering long-forgotten toys triggered gratitude for having so many fond memories to revisit. A box of old and regrettably moldy Kenner Building sets stirred childhood memories of building bridges and roads and housing developments, which made me grateful for having toys which involved assembling things. Rediscovering toy cars and dinosaurs and cowboys reminded me of the many flights of fantasy and imagination which they enabled. Finding plastic molded race cars and kazoos evoked fond memories of having made them in our Mattel VAC-

U-FORM, which made me feel grateful to have grown up in an age where kids could take more risks.

In much the same way, engaging with my own stuff also generated gratitude. Of course, revisiting memories associated with my things was easy so long as I kept them. Finding ways to keep my Preserving Memories mantra happy while letting go of things was an entirely different challenge. This required me to develop another set of strategies for letting go of stuff by generating self-rewarding gratitude:

Remembering and retelling stories -- Sometimes I took a moment to reminisce about an object I found by telling a story about my connection to it, either to myself or out loud if other people were around. Remembering these stories and feeling gratitude for the experiences they represented often removed the need to keep the physical object, and it turned the project into an extended trip down Memory Lane in the process. Old running shirts reminded me of the days when I could run faster (#383-384; trashed), while my collection of Great Peace March documents sparked memories of mid-1980s activism (#603; recycled). A cookie tin (#857; gift) evoked memories of eating more yummy Christmas cookies than I cared to count. Some old camping supplies recalled a weekend camping trip which I abandoned after getting totally soaked from an overnight rainfall that leaked into my tent (#933-937; trashed).

Capturing stories -- At times, it seemed necessary to capture a story instead of simply remembering it, so I wrote down a story which explained why I'd kept that object. Writing down these stories also made it easier to let the physical objects go, but I used this strategy more selectively because it would have taken too much time and effort to chronicle the story behind each object I encountered.

Taking pictures was another useful strategy for letting go of things because preserving memories by having an image of an object was usually just as good as having the physical object itself. This strategy worked well for artifacts that seemed to have memories worth preserving, such as the certificate of appreciation (#104) and a couple of old shirts commemorating a 100-mile bicycle ride and a 5K run (#770, 772; donated). Taking pictures also meant that I could also revisit them later, even if I rarely bothered to do this in practice.

Time travel was a mental trick I made up to help me put the value of something into perspective. The first time I used it was when I found a game from my childhood in my parents' garage which I hadn't seen or thought of in decades. It was like discovering a long lost friend; after so much time being separated from this game, how could I possibly get rid of it now? The trick was to remember the moment five minutes before rediscovering this game and all the moments in my life without remembering this game. Was my life a total waste until that moment? Would keeping this thing end some sort of prior deprivation and fill a hole in my life? The answer in this case, and in every other case when this happened, was that I was fine before rediscovering this object and would be fine without having it. The "time travel" strategy wasn't always enough by itself, but it worked well in combination with picture taking, storytelling, or culling.

None of the objects in my own home evoked memories that were quite so strong, but occasionally it was useful to do a less dramatic version of the time travel strategy when finding a forgotten object: Was I OK before I found this object? Would I be OK without having it? Some old art work (#585, 752-753; recycled), some papers from my teaching days (#751; recycled), and an old notebook from my youth (#965; recycled/trashed) fell into this category.

The Gratitude of Receiving

Beyond the gratitude I received from feeling good about giving things away to others, gratitude also resulted from receiving services, stories, strategies, and other non-physical things from other people during the project. It was especially easy to be grateful for the available services that made it easier to get rid of things. I was grateful for the various charities that offered home pickup service for donated items, the organizations that provided drop-off collection bins or boxes at various nearby locations, the online Freecycle group serving my local area, and the many Little Free Library kiosks scattered all over my town.

The process of clearing out my parents' house also made me grateful for the people who provided helpful services there. The most memorable example was someone who was known as Scrappy Pappy; he was the guy who came every so often to haul away the scrap metal which we had sorted out and put in garbage cans on the side of the house next to the garage. Many times, when I felt stuck trying to figure out what to do with yet another inscrutable metal object, I would simply say to myself the magic words "Scrappy Pappy!" and toss the thing into the metal recycling bin with a sense of relief. The mere thought of "Scrappy Pappy" made me happy.

Although I don't recall ever thinking about Scrappy Pappy during my project, I did collect objects in my own metal recycling bin throughout the summer and fall, so maybe his example was more influential than I realized. Eventually, the bin was full enough to make it worthwhile to take the 40-minute trip to the county dump. There, I recycled the metal (#570-578, #888-907, among others) along with some electronic equipment (#860-887). This made me grateful for being able to recycle so many things that had become useless to me or anyone else.

As I told more friends and colleagues about the 1,000 Things Project, some of them shared their own stories and strategies about getting rid of things in ways that generated gratitude. One of them told me that she kept a note on her attic door that said, "Who am I depriving by keeping this?" Each time she went to put something in the attic, the note would prompt her to think twice about keeping that thing rather than giving it to someone else who might find it useful. Another friend described how she donated some objects of historical value to a local museum, which was grateful to receive the items and add them to their collection.

My sister shared a story about giving something away that created an unexpectedly powerful form of gratitude. She initially had mixed feelings about how to get rid of a toy fire truck from my parents' house because it was worth a fair amount of money. She put it up for sale, and someone from the local fire company offered to buy it. They wanted to use the toy truck to let kids ride in it during the fire company's annual "hands-on" days. My sister liked knowing that kids would have fun riding in the same fire truck as we did when we were kids. But when the person from the fire company stopped by the house to look at the truck, my sister sold it for a very small amount of money instead, and only then because the person refused to take it for free. My sister's decision changed because that person had been to the house before; she was an emergency medical technician who had responded a couple of times to emergency calls for our mom, and she had revived her and helped her get to the hospital. The toy fire truck thus became a token of deep appreciation that my sister was more than grateful to pass on in this way.

A Cycle of Gratitude

Acts of gratitude, such as giving things away, revisiting and preserving memories, or receiving services, stories, and tips from others, generated energy for more acts of gratitude. This positive cycle of gratitude made it easier and more gratifying to let go of my things, and the mutual reinforcement of giving and receiving gratitude also helped power this cycle. Even though my efforts to give things away were far from automatic, doing this repeatedly formed a pattern over time which made it a little easier to give something away the next time. By paying attention to this cycle of gratitude, I soon discovered that there were also other positive cycles that I could use to help me let go of my stuff.

✣✣✣✣✣✣✣✣✣✣✣✣✣

Your Turn: How You Generate Gratitude

1) **Giving Things Away.** Name one or more object(s) that you have given away that has generated gratitude. How did the receiver feel grateful? How did you feel grateful?

2) **Your Strategies for Revisiting and Preserving Memories.** In the table on the next page, identify one or more objects you own for which you've taken the time to revisit and/or preserve their memories. For each object, identify which strategy(ies) you used for revisiting or preserving memories. If you wish, also briefly describe how it worked or didn't work for you and what happened to the object. (See first two columns for examples.)

3) **Receiving Gratitude**. Name two or more examples of non-physical things you have received (services, stories, strategies, or something else) for which you feel grateful and explain why you feel grateful for having received them.

Strategy(ies) You've Used for Revisiting/ Preserving Memories	My Examples of Objects		Your Example(s) of Objects	
	old running shirts (#383-384)	plastic toy storage bin (#600)		
Remembering Stories	✓			
Capturing Stories		✓		
Taking Pictures		✓		
Time Travel				
[others you've used]				
How It Worked/ What Happened	recycled them; remembered how I used to run faster	Freecycled; delivered to recipients' house		

Slow on the Inflow

Letting go of your stuff is also about more than just getting rid of stuff you already have.

When you spend time, energy, and attention focusing on what goes out of your home, sooner or later you'll start paying attention to what comes into your home as well. Once you start doing this, you're more likely to respond by slowing that inflow down. Although it may not make sense at first, this is actually another great way to learn how to let go of the stuff you already have because being slow on the inflow completes an important cycle which helps you let things go.

Completing the Cycle

"I don't get it."

I was on the phone with a friend trying to explain the 1,000 Things Project to him. 'What part do you not get?' I wondered to myself. I explained what I'd learned about how to let go of my stuff. I told him about the stories and inner voices, about treasures and possession, about curation and gratitude, and I told him that hundreds of things were gone from my house now as a result. He still didn't get it. We kept talking, and then I mentioned how I also wasn't buying nearly as much stuff as I had in the past. "Oh, I get it now," he said. "You're completing the cycle."

I'm doing what? Then, *I* got it; of course that's what I was doing. In a way, my friend understood my project better than I had; just letting things go wasn't enough. After all, what would be the point of letting things go if I simply replaced them with new stuff? How could I know the purpose or value of everything I owned if I brought new things into my home without knowing their purpose or value? My project made sense only because I'd also become much more careful about bringing stuff into my home. Being 'slow on the intake' enabled me to "complete the cycle," which in this case was a virtuous one.

Virtuous Cycles

There were various other cycles which I'd already discovered during the project. Some of these were vicious cycles that resulted from being too attached to stuff: cycles of possession, grasping, or other forms of attachment that fed on themselves, kept things in place, or even trapped me. Other cycles were positive, virtuous ones that resulted from being thoughtful about dealing with my belongings, such as the cycle of gratitude that generated positive energy by letting go of things. The collective effect of removing hundreds of objects created another virtuous cycle; the more things I let go, the more time, energy, and attention it freed up to deal with the things that remained. The flow of stuff into my house also created a virtuous cycle when I paid mindful attention to it.

Slow on the Intake: A Mindful Cycle

There wasn't as much stuff coming into my home as there had been before the project began, but there was a big difference between simply letting this happen and making it happen. Becoming 'slow on the inflow' really started to happen once I started making more mindful decisions about the intake of things into my home.

Before, my default setting for buying something was "Yes, if...," as in "Yes, I'll buy it if I want or need it"; cost was usually not the deciding factor since I could afford it in most cases. Being more mindful about buying new stuff shifted that setting to *"No, unless...,"* as in "**No** need to buy something **unless** I really need it." Saying No instead of Yes naturally slowed down the process of buying stuff, and it was also consistent with my project goals since it involved identifying the purpose or value of something before buying it.

"No, unless..." became my go-to strategy for slowing down the inflow of stuff into my home, which changed my intake behavior considerably in several ways. Not surprisingly, it resulted in my *buying less stuff, both new and used*. Being mindful about buying decisions meant thinking twice about them, which cut down on impulse purchases almost entirely. Reminding myself that someday I would have to get rid of any item I bought lessened my desire to buy things, as did considering the time, energy, and attention costs of ownership. I still bought new or used stuff now and then, but it happened far less frequently, and doing it more mindfully increased my satisfaction with the decisions and purchases I made.

Using the "No, unless" strategy to be slow on the intake was a little trickier when applying it to stuff I already owned. ***Getting full use out of stuff*** by deciding to keep it as long as it was useful delayed my replacing it with new stuff, and sometimes doing this made sense. Did I really need another pair of running shoes right away, or could I wait a little longer? Did I need to buy a new wheeled luggage bag just because there was a loose pin on the handle and the bottom was showing a little wear and tear, or could I make do with the bag as is? The danger with using this strategy was in holding onto some things for too long, such as the outdoor canopy chair (#671), but this danger was avoidable so long as I kept my focus on an object's purpose or value. For example, I finally trashed the chair because it was no longer usable, but I kept the wheeled luggage bag for several more years because it remained serviceable.

Becoming slow on the intake also changed my consumer habits, even though they weren't part of the project. For instance, ***being mindful about consumables*** changed my grocery shopping patterns. Since I was already buying fewer groceries as an empty nester, I gave myself permission to stock the kitchen with fewer food items instead of filling every empty shelf with groceries Just in Case. With fewer things to buy on each trip, I started paying more attention to the individual items I bought. This led me to resume using grocery lists more regularly, which helped me to simplify the choices I made. Having simpler choices made it convenient to shop less often at large supermarkets and start shopping more often at my local food co-op again. All of this helped me make healthier food choices while reducing the time, attention, and especially mental energy I spent on the grocery shopping process.

Being mindful about buying less stuff also changed some of my other consumer habits. I started using public services in place of buying things. Instead of buying books, I started using my local public library more often, both in person and online. Instead of using the car reflexively, I started doing some errands on foot and used public transportation more often, for instance taking the metro instead of driving to the airport. Taking the bus now and then, which I hadn't done in decades, provided a nice break from the stress of city driving, especially if I wasn't in a hurry.

All of these changes in my behavior resulted from the power of the *"No, Unless..."* strategy. It created a virtuous cycle of mindfulness which could be called "Mindful Out, Mindful In." Deciding to buy, consume, or otherwise acquire stuff is an act of reaching *out* into the world and bringing it *in* to one's life. Making these decisions mindfully by switching my approach from "Yes, if..." to *"No, unless..."* changed my buying choices so that I became slow on the intake when reaching out and taking in new things — mindful out, mindful in.

Becoming slow on the inflow was another big step forward in building a healthy relationship with my stuff. Using this virtuous cycle created genuine changes in how I thought, felt, and acted about bringing new physical objects into my home and my life. Very few things were still coming into my home mindlessly, and I was aware of the few instances when this still happened, for instance junk mail or the occasional mindless purchase which I didn't catch until after the fact. Even though the flow of new things into my house slowed considerably, I never felt deprived of anything. Instead, as I approached the end of my project, I now had a much greater awareness and more control over what came into my home, and I felt good about that.

✸✸✸✸✸✸✸✸✸✸✸✸✸

Your Turn: Being Slow on the Inflow

1) **Saying "No, Unless…"** Do you use a "No, Unless" strategy to control the flow of stuff into your home? If so, how and when do you use it? Do you have a different name for it? If so, what is it?

2) **Being "slow on the intake."** Are you being more careful about bringing new or used stuff into your home? Use the table below to identify how your behavior has changed, describe an example of what you've done and how it's worked or not worked for you.

How Your Behavior Changed	Example(s)	How That Worked/ Didn't Work for You
Buying less new stuff		
Buying less used stuff		
Keeping stuff longer		
Taking longer to replace stuff		
Changing consumer/ other habits		
Something else (describe)		

The Results

On January 11, I reached my target of 1,000 things after placing a book about Sun Tzu (#1,000; donated) into a Little Free Library box in my local community. (It was especially easy for me to donate this book after discovering that I had two of them.) This was 11 days later than planned, but my original target date had fulfilled its purpose of helping me reach my goal in a reasonable amount of time.

My project took eight months and required a considerable amount of time, energy, and attention over that period, so you may wonder if the results of a 1,000 Things Project are really worth the effort. The answer for me was a resounding yes. The project became an engaging journey of self-discovery, a process of (re)discovering the purpose and value of my possessions, and a path toward building a healthier relationship with my stuff. Here's where things went and how I did relative to reaching my original goals:

Where Things Went

I used the same legal-sized piece of paper to keep track of the 1,000 things throughout the entire project. It never occurred to me to use a spreadsheet or other digital file instead. I liked the immediacy of writing each thing down on paper and having the list to look at as a reminder or motivator. Here is how I got rid of the 1,000 things:

Recycling was my most common way to get rid of things. About 30 percent of them (282 in total), mostly paper, plastic, and metal objects, were completely recycled, and another 125 things were partly trashed and partly recycled, such as the conference badges and lanyards, the wrapping paper trash, the old tins of boot polish, and various other items.

Donations accounted for about 30 percent of the 1,000 things (293 in total), and they were the most effective way for me to get rid of a large number of things at one time. Although I didn't keep track of where specific items were donated during the project, reviewing my tax records at the end of the project enabled me to identify where most of the donations went, for instance:

- Vehicles for Change (old car, #153)
- Vietnam Veterans of America (clothing and other items, #154-283)
- Local optician's store (old glasses, #385-394)
- Local phone store (old cell phones, #395-400)
- Prevention of Blindness Society (various items, #675-707)
- Little Free Library (for example, Sun Tzu book, #1,000)

I also donated some books to the local public library and deposited some clothing and shoes into some nearby charitable collection bins.

Freecycling enabled me to get rid of about 5 percent of the 1,000 things (53 in total). Early in the project, Freecycling was my preferred way to get rid of things since I had already identified a number of items for disposal; almost 50 of the first 73 things were Freecycled. However, my use of Freecycling dropped off considerably after that as I ran short of items that were good candidates. Freecycling also required extra time and effort to manage the email communication and arrange pickup for each individual item, so at times it was less convenient to use.

Gifts were a relatively uncommon way to get rid of things (23 in total). Books were the most common gift along with a few odds and ends mentioned previously, such as the cookie tin, bundle of knitting supplies, and packing supplies.

About 20 percent of the 1,000 things (224 in total) ended up purely as *trash*, and another 125 things were partly trashed and partly recycled.

Having to throw hundreds of things into the trash showed how my house held a lot of unneeded junk and how keeping things Just in Case often didn't work out as intended.

A Less Cluttered Home

My home now *looked and felt noticeably less cluttered,* and that alone made the project worthwhile. Signs of progress were visible in many areas of the house. The dining room had a lot more open space, and the cabinet and storage chest in that room were now reasonably tidy. The kitchen counters, cabinets, and storage space above the cabinets were better organized and held far fewer objects. The living room and bedroom closets had more open storage space, and the home office upstairs had fewer bins and boxes on the floor. The main area of the basement showed the biggest improvement; there was much more open floor space, and the large nest of bins and boxes there had shrunken to a manageable size. My home also felt less cluttered because I had a pretty good sense of what things still remained at this point. While I didn't know exactly what was in every box or bin, I'd examined every part of my house, basement, and outdoor shed, and there were few surprises remaining to be encountered.

Insights and Lessons about Attachment

The 1,000 Things Project also gave me a wealth of *insights into my attachment to things.* The themes that emerged during the project — stories, inner voices, treasures, possession, gratitude, curation, slow on the inflow — became touchstones for describing the most important lessons I learned about holding on and letting go:

- Everything we own has a story to tell.
- Other inner voices, such as scripts and mantras, prescribe how we deal with our things.

- Many of the things we own are treasures worth keeping, but having too many things gets in the way of being able to enjoy, use, or appreciate the things we really want or need.
- Possession is a two-way street; so long as we own something, it also owns us.
- Possessions are anchors, keeping us in place and weighing us down.
- Our possessions take a lot more of our time, energy, and attention than we realize.
- Curation is a powerful practice for letting go of things by providing many useful strategies for thoughtfully deciding what to get rid of, keep, store, or display.
- Using the power of attachment by generating gratitude is a great way of letting things go.
- Becoming slow on the inflow by being more mindful about taking in things completes a cycle which helps us know the value or purpose of what we own.

Doing my project also revealed many other insights and lessons about attachment which you may also discover by doing your own project, for instance:

- Paying attention to how you hold on to things through stories, scripts, and mantras will help you figure out how to let them go.
- Amassing a lot of stuff without a purpose or value is really just a form of trash collection, an illusory "treasure" which will become someone else's trash once you're gone, their problem and their burden.
- Understanding the power of mutual possession will help you gain control of your relationship with your stuff.
- Identifying how your possessions anchor your life can help you decide which ones are benefiting you and which ones are keeping you stuck in place.

- Assessing the time, energy, and attention costs that your possessions demand from you will help you identify which things are worth the effort to keep.
- Letting go of stuff which is not worth the effort to keep releases more of your time, energy, and attention to be put to better use.
- Giving things away is almost always more satisfying than selling them, even in those rare cases where it may be possible to recover their monetary value.

You may also find, as I did, that there are no lingering attachments or regrets once you let something go. Any occasional regrets you may have will be minor and momentary. Eventually, it may be difficult to recall a single thing that you wished you'd kept; in most cases, you might even forget that you'd ever owned it. If you take pictures to help you let go of things, most likely you will rarely if ever even look at those pictures again. You may regret not having made better use of some of the things you get rid of, but you probably will never miss any of them.

Responsibly, Thoughtfully

My other project goals, and the structure of the project itself, enabled me to meet my goal to *do the process as responsibly and thoughtfully as possible*. Finding insights about my attachments to my stuff, seeking to build a healthy relationship with it, and identifying the purpose or value of individual items, all entailed being thoughtful. Counting to 1,000 was itself a thoughtful process, and naming my project after my target number helped me be responsible for meeting it.

Despite having to trash more things than I would have liked, I felt that I'd been as environmentally responsible as possible. Some things were clearly useless junk or otherwise not worth saving, and throwing away 50 CDs inflated the total of trashed items. Thinking like a museum curator helped me to be responsible by using culling strategies to figure out the purpose and value of my things. Mostly, being responsible was closely tied with making thoughtful decisions and an overall sense of intentional stewardship.

Being thoughtful about the process moved the project beyond clutter control and into the realm of building a healthier relationship with my stuff. The process started with paying attention to getting rid of things deliberately by taking a moment to engage with each item, listening for the stories, hearing the inner voices, and choosing a way to let go, instead of making a quick or thoughtless "snap" decision.

Being consistently thoughtful about the process increased my awareness about what my relationship with my possessions was really like: the role of scripts and mantras, the time, energy, and attention demands, the effects of having too much stuff getting in my life's way. Over time, this awareness transformed the process from a series of episodes and decisions into a practice which at times resembled a form of mindfulness. Dealing with my stuff often involved "a state of active, open attention to the present" that sometimes resulted in an "awakening to experience" and a more "heightened awareness." I could even be non-judgmental about my things now and then. While the project wasn't a mindfulness practice, it felt like one at times.

Being *thoughtful* can also remind you that being *thoughtless* about stuff is actually an essential part of our everyday lives. That may sound illogical, but in fact most of the stuff in our lives is designed to be acquired and used thoughtlessly. A multitude of labor-saving devices, everything from home appliances to prepared foods to vehicles to computers, saves us time and effort by reducing or eliminating the thought involved in using them. It would be mind-boggling to think about the details of where all that stuff comes from and even more overwhelming if we actually had to make everything we owned or consumed. This built-in thoughtlessness is precisely what enables us to enjoy what we have, but thoughtless consumption becomes a burden when an excess of accumulated stuff gets in the way of how we want to live and who we want to be.

Fortunately, you can also turn the power of thoughtlessness to your advantage. By dealing with your stuff thoughtfully and responsibly as a regular, repeated practice, eventually it becomes a habit, something you can do automatically without having to think about it. I found that this "thoughtless thoughtfulness" was a great antidote to the effects of past thoughtless consumption by freeing up physical, mental, and emotional space in my house, my mind, and my life.

A Healthier Relationship with My Stuff

Doing the project helped me *build a healthier relationship with my stuff* in many ways:

- *Listening to the stories, scripts and mantras my things had to tell me* was much healthier than ignoring them. Instead of following the scripts thoughtlessly, I could exercise more control over the process now that I was (back) in touch with my reasons for holding on to things. The occasional urge to blame myself for holding on to stuff disappeared once I understood the underlying reasons for it.
- *Identifying treasured objects* with clear value and purpose helped me distinguish between things that were healthy to keep and ones that were not.
- *Letting go of things without regret* became much easier for me, especially for the many things that were not worth the time, energy, and attention they demanded.
- *Discovering the curative power of curation* helped me appreciate more fully the things I decided to keep as a representative sample of my life stories and experiences.
- *Rediscovering the power of gratitude* made giving things away for others to have, use, and appreciate much more rewarding than holding on to them.

- *Becoming mindful about acquiring new items* helped me have less stuff without feeling deprived. Paying more attention to my consumer habits resulted in healthier lifestyle choices.
- *Doing this my way* was especially important. Structuring the project on my own terms gave me buy-in and ownership. It wasn't necessary to be hyper-organized, become a minimalist, or slavishly follow a method to have a healthy relationship with my stuff.

What Remained to Be Done

Doing the 1,000 Things Project was very satisfying, but work remained to be done. My ultimate goal of *living in a dwelling in which I can identify the purpose or value of everything I own* remained out of reach and out of sight. Plenty of things remained in my house that no longer had real purpose or value to me, but I hadn't yet figured out how to let go of them, or I simply hadn't gotten to them yet. There were still nests in the dining room, in bins on the floor of the office, and in numerous other places. The closets, office, basement, and most other areas of the house still needed more culling. There was so much left to do that I couldn't really tell how much farther I had to go to reach this goal.

A lot of questions also remained about how much more progress I could make on my other goals. My house still had plenty of clutter; how much less cluttered would it be if culling and curating became a regular practice? What new insights would I learn from going through the nests and stashes of things that remained untouched during the project, including the ones that I'd "organized" before the project began? How much healthier could my relationship with my stuff become if I got better at managing my inner voices that at times still ran the show? Could I allow myself to let go of some mementos or other treasures that I hadn't yet touched? Could I get better at generating gratitude more proactively by giving things away more often? Were there ways to make it even easier to be thoughtful about the process? Would the process improve if I practiced more regularly the strategies I'd discovered?

Clearly it would take a lot more work to answer all these questions and to find out what it would really be like to know the value or purpose of everything I owned. This meant that it was time to make another, easier decision: Would I do a second 1,000 Things Project? The answer was yes — and maybe more.

❈❈❈❈❈❈❈❈❈❈❈❈❈

Your Turn: Your Results

If you've done a 1,000 Things Project:
- What results did you get? Which of your goals did you reach (or not)?
- What did you learn from your project? What were the most valuable lessons that you learned, and why were they valuable to you?
- How has your relationship with your stuff changed as the result of doing your project? Would you describe it as healthier? Why or why not? How else would you describe the change(s) in your relationship with your stuff?

If you haven't (yet) finished a 1,000 Things Project:
- Read the section in the Getting Started chapter, "Your Turn: Getting Started with Your Project" for tips on starting your project.
- Read the section in the next chapter, "Your Turn: Getting Going (Again) with Your Project" for tips on getting your project re-started.
- Keep on reading this book until you are ready to begin your own project in your own way.

Part IV: Getting Better, Getting Good

Starting a Second Project

There may be other ways to find out the value or purpose of everything one owns, but doing a second 1,000 Things Project was the way I chose. It wasn't at all clear that doing a second project would actually get me all the way there, but perhaps it would put me within sight of my goal at least. Besides, I was already on a roll since I'd gotten rid of 21 additional items on the last day of the first project. It'd be a shame to let that head start go to waste, so I got out another sheet of legal size, yellow lined paper and wrote a title for this new project at the top. The "2nd 1000 Things Project: 1000 things in < 6 months" reflected my intention to do the second project more quickly than the first one. I used the same ground rules as for the first project:

- Keeping a list of items I got rid of in numerical order, including the disposal method and date;
- Defining a "thing" as any individual entity which required my time, energy, or attention;
- Using the same target number of 1,000 because it still appealed to me for the same reasons as before (large round number, big enough to make a difference, small enough to be attainable);
- Expecting the process to require substantial effort and commitment, a target timeline, multiple goals, and a combination of planning and adapting as I went along.

My plan for this time around was to apply what I'd learned during the first project, practice more regularly the strategies I'd learned, and find some new strategies as well. I figured that doing this would help me let go of things more easily and quickly, make more progress toward my goals, and prepare me to deal with the more difficult stuff that lay ahead.

Another Start, Another Surge, Another Slog

My second 1,000 Things Project began a lot like the first one. Thanks in part to my 21-item head start, I got rid of 71 things in the first week, even more than the 65 I'd gotten rid of in the first week of my first project. It was a lot of little things mostly: various books (#1,002-1,006; donated), some used compact fluorescent bulbs (#1,022-1,038; recycled), lots of old papers culled from work and school folders (#1,042-1,045, 1,049-1,068; recycled), and some old soccer, tennis, and rubber balls (#1,069-1,071; trashed). By the end of the first month, though, my tally was 110, lagging well behind the 283 things I'd gotten rid of during the first project. The initial surge was smaller, and the pace started lagging sooner. This slog seemed bigger somehow, and I started to wonder, *'Not again — what's happening this time?'*

One reason for my slower progress was that I started a personal blog to record my thoughts about the project and to find out if people were interested in knowing more about it. The process of reflecting on, remembering, and recording what had already happened during the first project while doing the second one added more time and effort to the entire endeavor. Other life events, such as work-related trips, often took priority and pushed this project aside for periods of time.

Another big reason was that most of the easy stuff was gone by this point; many of the things that remained had stronger attachments and were more difficult to part with. The energy that comes from doing something new was also missing the second time around, and simply applying what I'd already learned wasn't having as much of an effect as I'd hoped.

Once again, doing more of the same wasn't doing it for me anymore. My project needed a jolt of new energy from somewhere. It wasn't enough simply to have strategies or want to use them more regularly or continue to discover new ones. My journey needed to change and so it did, this time from a process of discovery to a focus on how to be strategic.

Getting Better by Being Strategic: The Process

The process of chronicling what had already happened during the first project was an easy way for me to focus on process. The remainder of this book will focus mainly on process as well because *the way to get better at building a healthy relationship with your stuff is to be strategic about the process*. It all starts with paying thoughtful attention more strategically. Counting is a useful strategy for doing this because it provides an easy way to set a goal, keep track of progress, and measure progress over time. It allows for flexibility in choosing time periods and quantities in both the short and long term. It also provides an effective way of valuing each thing you encounter by taking the time to count it at the very least before disposing of it.

Beyond counting, there are several other ways that you can pay thoughtful attention to the process of being strategic:

Figure out how you are already good at being strategic. Start by paying attention to how you are currently being strategic. Here are three ways of doing this that worked for me:

1) **Identify what you already do to be strategic**. In my case, I recorded an inventory of strategies that I'd discovered and used during the first project, such as strategies for getting started, for culling, and for generating gratitude (see Appendix for a detailed chart).

You can use this list to identify what you already do to be strategic, and you can also update this inventory of the strategies you use as you go along. Of course, you can also make your own inventory of strategies; it requires a little time, energy, and attention at first, but it takes little effort to maintain once you have it.

2) **Identify when and how often you are strategic.** Pay attention to when you are being strategic and when you are not, then observe how you respond to that. What do you like about how you're currently being strategic? What do you wish to change?

It's also useful to notice how often you use various strategies. Some strategies I only used now and then; in other words, I *applied* them sometimes. Other strategies I used regularly or often, but I still had to think consciously about using them; in other words, these strategies had become *practices*. Then there were strategies that I found myself using automatically without having to think about them; these strategies had become *habits*.

3) **Figure out which strategies are already practices and habits for you.** Distinguishing between *application, practice,* and *habits* also helped me figure out which strategies I did well and were easy to use. In my case, various culling strategies had already become regular practices, while being thoughtful, counting, and severely restricting the flow of new things into my home (*"No, Unless"*) had become habits. Your experience may be different.

Figure out how you could get better at being strategic. Here are three ways that worked for me:

1) **Figure out which strategies you could do more often**. The distinctions between application, practice, and habits can be useful here as well. Which strategies could you apply often enough to become a regular practice? Which regularly practiced strategies could turn into useful habits? What new strategies would you like to try

out? The following chapters will describe how this turned out for me; again, your experience may be different.

2) **Figure out which strategies you could use more effectively.** Pay attention to which strategies work well for you and when. Which strategies are reliable, go-to ones? Which ones don't really work well for you, and why? Which ones work some of the time but not others? What factors determine when strategies work well and when they don't? What could you change to make them work more effectively for you?

3) **Keep discovering new strategies.** Keep paying attention to the process of doing the project, and you will also discover new strategies as you go along.

Each of these ways of paying thoughtful attention to the process of being strategic will help you get better at it. "Learning by doing" through self-discovery is a great way to learn, but there's no need to limit yourself to learning from your own project experience. There are many other resources that have a lot to offer, and at this point in my own journey, it was time for me to start learning from them.

❖❖❖❖❖❖❖❖❖❖❖❖

Your Turn: Getting Going (Again) with Your Project

How's your journey going?

Maybe you're now ready to get started on your first project; if so, you can review the Getting Started section in Part 1 of this book for a few tips on starting your project. You can also always go back to the Your Turn sections in previous chapters as well the ones in upcoming chapters.

Maybe you've already finished a project and are getting ready to start another one. If so, congratulations! Now's a good time to ask yourself how you want your next project to be relative to the previous one. What do you want to keep on doing in your next project? What do you wish to change? Maybe you're ready to figure out how to get better at the process and make your relationship with your stuff that much healthier. In that case, you might find this part of the book to be especially helpful.

Maybe you've decided to take a little break from working on your relationship with your stuff, which is fine. It can help to step back and take stock of where your journey has taken you — where you are now relative to reaching your goals or setting new ones, how far you've come from where you started, and what the next chapter of your journey might be.

Or, maybe you're having trouble getting started again, which is also common. Every relationship journey has its ups and downs. During a 1,000 Things Project, you will likely experience periods where your energy is high, the process flows easily, and progress seems to come quickly, as it did for me during the start of my first and second projects. You will also experience times that feel like a slog, where your energy is low, the process feels exhausting, and progress comes slowly, as it felt for me soon after the start of my first and second projects.

The best way to deal with slogs in my experience is to accept them as part of the process, try different strategies to re-energize your process, and muddle through them as best you can. Different strategies work at different times for different people, so try out some of the strategies listed in the Appendix or use the tips in this book's Getting Started section to help you get going again. It also helps to remember that your journey to build a healthy relationship with your stuff is a process, not a race, and that you control the process; it does not control you. Take breaks as you need them, and resume when you're ready.

Learning from Others

Learning intentionally from other people's experiences is another great way to be strategic about the process of building a healthy relationship with your stuff. Three particularly helpful approaches you can use are to collect strategies and ideas from other people, collect strategies from reading books on the topic, and use what you learn to personalize your experience. Using these approaches will enable you to:

- Confirm the value of the specific strategies and overall approach you are using;
- Find ways to improve the strategies you already use;
- Discover new strategies and ideas that you would have never thought of yourself; and
- Figure out how to adapt these strategies in ways that make sense to you.

Here's how I used these approaches to learn from others.

Collecting Strategies from Other People

During my first project, I'd started mentioning it to other people on purpose to see how they would react, and a lot of them were eager to share their ideas about how to do such a project. Soon after starting the second project, I began to make a conscious effort to collect these ideas by sharing my own stories in casual conversations with friends, family, colleagues, and the occasional random stranger. Sometimes I would ask them directly to share any strategies they used for their own decluttering process, but more often than not, they would simply share some of their strategies without my asking. Almost everyone had strategies to share, and many of them were so good that I started carrying around a little notebook to record them. Here are some that were particularly useful:

Red/Yellow/Green — A friend of mine used this strategy for making a first pass through stuff. The strategy is simple: identify a particular area, such as a closet, box, drawer, or other nests, and simply sort the items quickly into three categories: Red (= keep), yellow (= not sure yet), and green (= OK to let go). The key to making the strategy work is to decide quickly without much thought. Although this may sound like the opposite of being thoughtful, in reality this "quick cull" approach is simply a way of conserving your time, energy, and attention by tapping into your own intuition quickly. The inner voices and storytelling are still there, but you bypass the "extended play" version and simply hear the opening line: "Keep me!" (red); "Time for me to go…" (green); "Let me tell you why…" (ok, yellow). If you find yourself spending more time on the decision, then it's probably for a good reason, and that's when being thoughtful comes into play.

Red/Yellow/Green eventually became one of my go-to strategies, especially when I was having trouble getting started or had a limited amount of energy for the task. Many times, most of the items I sorted through ended up in the yellow pile, but that was OK because I had also sorted out my keepers (red pile) and things to let go (green pile), so the original pile would be that much smaller when I tackled it again, thoughtfully, the next time. Sometimes, very few items ended up in the yellow pile, for instance when I was sorting through papers or clothing.

Use decluttering as therapy — A friend of mine described to me how she had spent a few hours in her home cleaning out a closet that had been bothering her. When she was done, she felt so much better that she described the process as a therapy session.

Sometimes, you just need to take a break from working on the relationship and drop down into clutter control mode for a while, and decluttering as therapy is a great way to do just that. Imagine the clutter in your home as a convenient collection of therapy sessions-in-waiting; the "office" is right there, and you can make an appointment whenever you choose. Decluttering therapy sessions are also low cost (the only cost is your time, energy, and attention) and effective (imagine that feeling of release as you look at a space that you've liberated from clutter).

After hearing my friend's story, I often found myself experiencing my decluttering efforts as therapeutic. Whether it's cleaning out a closet, emptying the outbox in your office, or sorting through your stash of saucepans in the kitchen, using decluttering as therapy can be a great remedy for dealing with the disorder of a cluttered home.

Remove the guilt — This is an attitude-based strategy which I learned from a friend of mine who was especially concerned about how her possessions might burden her children when she passed away. She felt that expecting her children to be the keeper of her stuff was an unfair way to impose guilt on them, so the heart of this strategy is to remove the guilt by detaching the object from the person who's associated with it. As she put it, "Getting rid of Grandma's table doesn't mean getting rid of Grandma." A related strategy she used was to **have a succession plan** for stuff you plan to keep but don't want to have just tossed out once you're gone. For instance, she has a succession plan for all her knitting stuff that identifies which things each recipient will inherit when she passes away.

Collecting Strategies from Books on the Topic

My first project seemed so personal that it never even occurred to me to read any books on decluttering or related topics then. Several months into the second project, I was ready to see what I could learn from reading books that would help me get better at the process. An Amazon Kindle book search on the terms "clutter" and "decluttering" found a huge number of books on the topic, and a quick perusal through the catalog of results revealed several themes motivating this mini-genre, such as *'have less stuff,' 'be minimalist about your stuff,'* or *'become organized.'* Not surprisingly, there were often differences of opinion about best approaches, for instance whether it's better to despise clutter and disorganization or to tolerate it. Some books promoted connections that would have never occurred to me, such as one between decluttering and weight loss (lose your stuff, lose your spare tire).

The most attractive theme to me was *"change your life"* because it seemed to fit well with what I was already doing. My project goals were all ways of making changes to my life. Many of these books appeared to be promoting a much grander, capital letter Change Your Life scope of change. My journey felt more like lower case change. but the theme fit well even if the scope did not, so I picked five books to read that related to this theme: *The Life-Changing Magic of Tidying Up* (hereafter *Tidying Up*); *SHED Your Stuff, Change Your Life* (*SHED*); *Letting Go: The Tao of Decluttering* (*Letting Go*); *Breathing Room: Open Your Heart by Decluttering Your Home* (*Breathing Room*); and *The Zero Waste Home* (*Zero Waste*). I bought digital versions of these five books and read them over the summer with two main purposes in mind: to find strategies, tips, and other ideas from the books that would help me get better at getting rid of my stuff and to find out what was different about my approach relative to theirs.

Reading these books confirmed the value of the specific strategies and overall approach I was using, for example:

- All of the books noted the need to distinguish between stuff that's valuable and stuff that's not by identifying treasured things, curating collections, and letting go of stuff that lacks value.
- The advice to "listen to your clutter" as it tells us "about our attachments, fears… [and] regrets about missed opportunities or our

disappointments in life" (*Breathing Room*) reminded me of the inner voices that had become such a defining presence in my own projects.
- The notion that clutter can weigh you down and become an obstacle in your life (*Breathing Room*) echoed my discoveries about how possessions can be anchors.
- The assertion that decluttering is also about learning how to refrain from collecting stuff in the first place (*Zero Waste*) affirmed my "No, Unless..." strategy as a way to make this happen.

The books also offered tips that helped me improve some of the strategies I was already using, for instance:

- The notion of identifying objects that have completed their role in your life, acknowledging their contribution, saying thank you, and letting them go with gratitude (*Tidying Up; Letting Go*) appealed to me. I found that this strategy worked particularly well with letting go of books (also see the Culling as Habit chapter later in this book for more details).
- *Zero Waste* included useful sections to help with systematically reducing the clutter in various areas of one's home, especially difficult nest areas. The section on bedroom cabinets included a detailed checklist of questions to ask during the downsizing process, such as whether or not an item is in working condition, used regularly, or worth the effort to maintain.
- *Letting Go* offered useful and more specific insights about the time, energy, and attention costs of our possessions, as captured in this description of how a piece of clothing can "own" us:

> If it was a popular name brand, you might have had to work five hours or more [to pay] for that dress...What better activities could you have done with that five hours?...This is precisely how what you own, owns you. That dress owns five hours of your time...Look into your closet— How much time is in there? [Loc. 228, Kindle version]

Reading these books also showed me how my approach was different from theirs in several important ways, such as structuring my journey as a project, counting as a way of measuring progress, and focusing on goals beyond clutter control, in particular building a healthy relationship with my stuff. This also confirmed the value of the specific strategies and overall approach I was using because it reinforced the value of *doing the project my way*. Each of the books I read was overly prescriptive about how to get rid of one's stuff, and their particular methods or approaches were often at odds with my preferences, for example:

- Telling you how many books to keep or how many shirts or pairs of shoes to have when those were decisions I wanted to make for myself.
- Disengaging your identity from your stuff when I was much more interested in mining, curating, and drawing strength from my identity through my stuff.
- Turning your decluttering project into a spiritual journey when I preferred to define the meaning of my journey on my own terms.
- Defining the meaning of your stuff in terms of narrow criteria rather than using a concept of purpose and value that included a much broader range of criteria, such as security, safety, comfort, satisfaction, utility, and giving.

Of course, doing your project your way could mean following someone else's method. Chances are, though, that sooner or later you'll find yourself deviating from that method, which fortunately is another great way of learning from others.

Personalizing What You Learn

Whether you encounter strategies while following a method or discover them on your own, you can *personalize* what you learn by using these strategies in ways that make sense to you. For example, some methods prescribe the strategy of **going through your stuff by category** (books, clothes, mementos, etc.), but this strategy might not always work well for you. (Trying to use this strategy exclusively didn't work for me, although it was useful on occasion.) The same might be true with **going through your stuff by spatial area,** such as a corner of a room, closet, or shelf of boxes. You might find it more useful to **mix spatial and categorical sessions** instead; sort through your stuff by spatial area one session, then go through it by category the next time. Using both options creates more variety, and counting the items you get rid of is a way to measure progress.

You might also discover strategies from outside the realm of decluttering that you can apply usefully to your project. For instance, I struggled with using time boundaries as a decluttering strategy until I adapted an idea from the world of software development and started to **do decluttering in sprints**. The term "sprint" refers to a set period of time of focused work on a project, often with the goal of completing a specific set of work. A decluttering "sprint workout" can use a numerical goal, such as getting rid of x number of things or preparing y number of things for "disposal," or it can focus on a particular small area, such as a drawer or the contents of a shelf or box, within a given time period. The metaphor of "sprints" can help you to focus on doing decluttering quickly for a relatively short period of time, and it also helps to remind you that recovery time is sometimes needed before running another sprint. Doing sprints helps with managing time, energy, and attention while avoiding burnout from the decluttering process.

Learning from others is a great way to collect new strategies, and personalizing how you use them increases their effectiveness. The experience of learning from others can also help you get better at discovering new strategies on your own along the way.

✼✼✼✼✼✼✼✼✼✼✼✼

Your Turn: How You Learn from Others

1) **Learning from Other People:** What strategies have you learned from talking with other people about your own decluttering project? Which ones have been especially valuable, and how have you used them? Which ones have become regular practices? Habits?

2) **Learning from Reading Books:** What strategies have you learned from reading other books about decluttering? Which ones have been especially valuable, and how have you used them? Which ones have become regular practices? Habits?

3) **Personalizing What You've Learned:** What strategies have you personalized and made your own? How did you do this?

Tuning in to Healthy Talk

Inner Voices Redux

You may have noticed that the process of dealing with your stuff affects your internal dialogue, especially once you've gotten rid of a lot of things. The stories, scripts, mantras, and self-talk that appear when you're deciding what to do with your things start to change, and your reactions may change as well. For starters, you may wonder why those inner voices are still around in the first place. Shouldn't they have gone away by now? Or be a little more quiet at least?

The reality is that *inner voices don't go away.* They are always there for most items whether you choose to hear them or not, and they don't get more quiet either. In fact, they become *stronger and louder than ever*, especially once you've gotten rid of the easier things and start dealing with stuff which has stronger attachments. Your inner critic is probably still annoyingly noisy as well.

Not only that, but the *inner voices also become more numerous and varied.* In my case, dealing with more difficult things meant encountering new inner voices to add to my growing chorus. I couldn't tell whether they were really new or whether I was simply getting better at hearing them, but there were more of them either way.

Even after you've dealt with thousands of your things, *some familiar inner voices remain.* You're likely to continue hearing many of the same scripts, such as *It might be worth something; I can't just throw it out*, or *I paid a lot for that; I can't just give it away,* among others. **Sometimes they change their tune,** expressing subtle variations of their usual messages, for instance: *You paid a lot of money for that [x]. You can't just give it away to* *someone you don't know*. (Also see examples in Appendix and later in this chapter.)

At times, these inner voices can feel like obstacles to be overcome or a problem that needs fixing, but the reason that your internal dialogue doesn't go away is because that's how *you communicate with yourself about your relationship with your stuff*. This conversation ultimately begins and ends with you, and your stuff serves as the medium for this communication to happen. This communication isn't always easy or healthy; inner voices can often be stubborn, resistant to change, or even self-defeating, which is why getting better at communicating with your inner voices becomes an even more important part of the process.

Fortunately, being strategic about dealing with your internal dialogue changes how you deal with your stuff, and vice versa. As with any relationship, good communication is one of the key elements of a healthy relationship with your stuff, and the way to establish good communication strategically is to learn how to turn your internal dialogue into *healthy talk*. Making healthy talk is about communicating with yourself effectively by talking, listening, and expressing your values, needs, and preferences through your internal dialogue. Tuning in to this 'healthy talk' helps you get better at the process of building a healthy relationship.

Strategies for Tuning in to Healthy Talk

Tuning in to healthy talk begins with **paying attention** to the inner voices you hear whenever you are deciding what to do with one of your things. Focus on hearing the stories first; simply looking at the object for a short time will usually prompt a story or a rush of stories. If that doesn't happen, try to **activate the storytelling** by asking yourself questions about that object and listening for the answers. When and where did you get it? How have you used it? Where have you traveled with it? What's the most memorable event that comes to mind when you look at this object?

Then, listen for the script(s) that tell you why you have that object and what to do with it. If you want to let the object go, but the script(s) are getting in the way, you might need to **change the script** first, as I learned to do during the first project and continued to do during the second one. An easy way to change the script is to check the existing script for outdated, questionable, or otherwise bad reasons for holding on to something, and then change the script by integrating gratitude, culling, or other strategies for letting go into the existing one. Here are a few examples of scripts that I changed during the first project (old scripts in italics; new scripts in parentheses):

- *'It could be worth something Some Day.'* (How much could it be worth? Is it worth the time, energy, and attention it will take to hold onto it? If not, let it go.)
- *'I paid a lot of money for it; I can't just give it away.'* (Yes, I can; I got my money's worth. It's a sunk cost at this point; give it away and create gratitude.)
- *'I have fond memories of that event; I can't just throw out that ticket/badge/program.'* (Sure I can; just take a picture or tell a story about it first, or simply have one more remembrance of this moment in my past and then allow it to pass on.)

As the scripts became more varied and subtly more challenging during the second project, I had to get better at finding ways to change them. For example, encountering a punctured balance ball evoked the script: *'You paid a lot of money for that; you can't just throw it away. Maybe try fixing it.'* I tried patching the leaks but without success, so I changed the script to "I paid some money for this, but I got some good use out of it, and I can't fix it. It's OK to throw it away" (#1,095; trashed). I heard a simpler version of this script for things that didn't cost a lot of money: *'It'd be a shame to just throw it away. Maybe try fixing it.'* A similar change of script ("No, I really can't fix it, and it's not worth the time and effort for me to try. It's OK to throw it away") helped me let go of several other items, such as a torn work glove (#1,096; trashed), a small alarm clock with the back missing (#1,097; trashed), and a couple of old bicycle tubes (#1,406-1,407; trashed). A rain barrel evoked a surprisingly sticky mix of scripts: *'You bought this from someone else and paid $10 for it. Maybe you'll start gardening again Some Day and then you'll be glad you have it. Best hold on to it Just in Case.'* But after several years of disuse, it was time to change the script: "I haven't used it, and I don't plan to start gardening again. Better to give it away to someone who will actually use it" (#1,502; Freecycled).

As you deal with more difficult items, you will likely encounter new, more challenging scripts where simply changing the script once might not be enough. Instead, you might need to change it more than once or even change it so much that in effect you're **writing a new script.** This happened to me with a twin bed which had been stored in my basement for several years. It had provided many greatly appreciated years of use, but it had long since served its purpose, and yet I still held on to it. At first, the bed evoked a familiar inner voice: *'Maybe someone in your family could use it. You can't just give it away to someone you don't know.'* Never mind that no one in my family lived nearby or had ever expressed any need for a bed — *'but maybe Some Day.'* When I first tried to change that script to "No one in your family needs it; it's OK to give it away to someone you don't know," a more subtle version took its place: *'You paid a lot of money for that bed. You can't just give it away to someone you don't know.'* Hmmm — so it's OK to give away items with some monetary value to family members but not to total strangers? I didn't quite understand where this notion came from, but this new wrinkle stopped me in my tracks for a while. Then someone told me about a local charity that accepted donations of household goods which went directly to needy families. Somehow the idea that the bed would be put to immediate use helped me rewrite the script: *'I can give away something to someone I don't know, even if I paid a lot of money for it, if I think about how much it might be useful to them.'* This new, improved script helped me donate the bed

(#1,286) and also give away several other items with some monetary value, such as a cross-country ski trainer (#1,506; Freecycled) and a circular saw (#1,849; Freecycled).

Another effective strategy is to **listen for new, healthier scripts** that come to you on their own. For instance, during the second project I went to an outdoor expo that had lots of tents and exhibits with brochures and other goodies for visitors to take away with them. Usually, if I saw an interesting brochure, I would reflexively pick it up and take it home, but this time, my inner voices told me an unexpectedly different message: *'I could get the information from their website. If I take the brochure with me, I'll just file it away somewhere and then forget about it for years. If it's really important to me, I'll use this moment as a reminder to go look at the website; I don't need the brochure to remind me of this.'*

And it worked! I put the brochure back, and after returning home, I visited the website and re-accessed the information there; my need for a physical brochure had disappeared. This new script was also useful for getting rid of numerous other brochures I'd collected previously, such as a Snapchat brochure (#1,416), a martial arts brochure (#1,359), and various travel brochures (#1,350-1,358, 1,781; all recycled).

You can also *gather new healthy scripts* from other sources, including books, other people, and your own past experience. They are easy to find once you start looking for them. Here are some of the ones I started using:

- "Thank you for the role you have played in my life…Time for you to go and make some new stories somewhere else."
- "We can treasure this [person, place, memory] in other ways without having to keep [object]."
- "Figure out how much time I am saving by not buying this [x]."

Healthy Self-Talk

The quality of your internal dialogue about your project itself is important too, so it's helpful to pay attention to it. Monitor the messages you're telling yourself. Are they constructive, affirming messages, or negative, self-defeating ones? What is their tone and substance, and how do you feel about what they are saying?

During my first project, I simply observed and noted examples of this internal dialogue about the project itself once I started noticing it. During the second project, I started to deal with this form of internal dialogue more strategically, and you can do the same in these ways:

Talk to yourself about your progress relative to your goals. Focus on what you've accomplished, and include what you have yet to accomplish in a way that serves you. *'Almost 100 things this week! That's moving me much closer to my goal.' 'This room is almost free of clutter! It's almost hard to remember when I could barely walk in here not that long ago.'*

Give yourself some simple affirmations now and then. *'Good work!' 'I did it!' 'Well done!' 'Having this closet culled is reward enough, but I'll go reward myself again anyway…'*

Acknowledge negative self-talk when it happens. Your inner critic may re-emerge now and then to question the value of the project (*'…This is still a waste of time. This is not worth the effort anymore…'*) or to take more potshots at you (*…'Yep, you are **definitely** weird for doing this. You've gone off the deep end on this one…'*) This is another occasion where rewriting the scripts can be very helpful, for instance: "Actually, this is well worth the effort because look at how much more space there is in the dining room … lots of nests are now completely gone … I can see the floor in my office again."

Another strategy is to **externalize some of your internal dialogue** in the form of journaling, blog posts, or conversations with others. Inner voices have a curious ability to sound rational and sensible while inside our minds, but they often sound not so rational and sensible anymore when they are put into print or shared with others.

Turning your internal dialogue into healthy talk becomes especially important once you're making decisions more often about more difficult items. If you keep tuning in to your healthy talk regularly, it will eventually become a habit, one of several habits which will serve you well when dealing with the more difficult stuff.

✳ ✳ ✳ ✳ ✳ ✳ ✳ ✳ ✳ ✳ ✳ ✳ ✳ ✳

Your Turn: Your Healthy Talk

1) **Your Healthy Talk Strategies.** Use the table below to identify which "healthy talk" strategies you have used for dealing with your inner voices, Include one more examples of ones that have become regular practices and/or habits. Add any new strategies you've found or created during your journey.

Strategy	Used	Practice	Habit	Example(s)
Active listening				
Storytelling				
Changing the script				
Write new scripts				
Gather new healthy scripts from others				
Listen for/hear healthy new scripts				
Healthy meta/self-talk				

2) **Dealing with Your Scripts.** Which scripts have you heard when sorting through your stuff? How did you respond? If you kept the item, why? If you let it go, what new scripts(s) did you use to support your decision? Use the table on the next page to record your results.

Include any other notable scripts you've heard or new ones you've created during your journey.

Script	Item(s), Decision(s)	New Script(s)
'It might be worth something (Some Day); I can't just throw it out'		
'I paid a lot for that; I can't just give it away'		
'My [family member] might want that some day'		
'I might want to look through those (papers, pictures, etc.) some day'		
'This was so-and-so's favorite'		
'I have fond memories of that event; I can't just throw out that [memento].'		

Culling as Habit:
Tackling the Tough Stuff

Many of the items you own often have strong attachments because they may have had a special purpose, utility, or value to you, such as storing important information, chronicling a memorable period of your life, or embodying your sense of self. You may be re-encountering collections of things which you passed over the first or second time around but can't overlook any longer. Decisions become more difficult once you start tackling this tough stuff. The stories you encounter may be stronger and more compelling; the inner voices you hear may be more insistent, and their underlying scripts may be new and more challenging. Among the strategies you can use to sort through your stuff, culling strategies are often the most powerful ones for dealing with these more difficult items. Tackling the tough stuff often means that it's time to do some serious culling, and maybe even make a habit out of it.

Culling as Habit

Culling strategies work well with most types of items, and using various culling strategies became a regular habit for me during my second project. Now and then, I could still *find some easy stuff to start with*, such as a pile of rags (#1,497-1,501; trashed) and a couple of belts (#1,571-1,572; trashed) which had worn out from heavy use. I *exterminated a few small collections* of beach bag junk (#1,486-1,493; trashed), plastic plumbing joints (#1,511; gave bag to local hardware store), and Halloween stuff (#1,921-1,941; Freecycled). My collection of thermoses and water bottles were prime candidates for *thinning out the herd*, as I selected a few to keep and gave the rest of them (#1,517-1,521) to someone else. I also thinned out my collections of linens (part of #1,098-1,124) and clothing (part of #1,599-1,667) by selecting unneeded ones and donating them to local charities.

Paper Life

Combining culling strategies with other types of strategies can also be helpful when tackling the tough stuff, and this is especially true with one particular type of stuff. Doing a 1,000 Things Project is a great way to realize how much of the stuff you own is made of paper. In my case, almost 30 percent (285) of the first 1,000 things were made of paper, and the variety of their forms was truly remarkable: magazines (#99-101), a poster board (#102), a certificate of appreciation (#104), wrapping paper trash (#106), wall posters (#300-303), conference badges (e.g., #427-466), prospectuses (#523-538; #778-782), business cards (#542-569), old calendars (#583-584), and a school handbook (#783), among others. During the second project, an even larger proportion of the things I let go of were made of paper — well over half of them (531 to be more exact). Sorting through my Paper Life was really how the practice of culling became a habit. I encountered an even wider variety of paper objects during the second project, including an old checkbook (#1,281), various user guides and warranty information (e.g., #1,523-1,535), old art work (e.g., #1,700-1,709, 1,800-1,805), and an expired International Driving Permit (#1,909). Most of my paper objects, though, were in the form of documents, folders, some maps, and lots of books, and they could be tough to deal with because each of these types posed its own special set of challenges.

Office Paper was a huge part of my Paper Life, especially since I ran a consulting business out of my home for almost 20 years. If you have clear goals and an organized collection of documents, it can be relatively easy to get rid of office paper. In my case, my goals were to have an office where I could find things simply whenever I needed them and where there were no storage bins sitting on the floor. Most of my documents were relatively well-organized at this point, so I didn't have to spend much time and energy on doing that.

Even so, sorting through paper documents can be challenging. Lots of papers are important for record-keeping purposes or have some other value. File folders full of papers can function just like little nests, a mix of valuable documents and ones that are no longer needed. Many file folders require looking at each piece of paper to decide whether to keep it, let it go, or convert it to digital form. Most of all, there is often just a lot of paper, period!

Fortunately, *starting with easy stuff, thinning out the herd,* and *idea mining* are strategies that work well with office paper, and they are often even easier to use when combined with other strategies. One way to find easy stuff while also culling by spatial area is to *pick a discrete location or object,* such as a specific bin or file cabinet drawer, or you can pick a smaller unit, such as a single outbox tray or even just one manila file folder at a time. Many people also find it motivating to *organize an area while culling it*. Using *sprints* can also be very effective; in my case, I preferred short time periods (one or two hours at most) and did not set numerical targets very often, especially since office paper can be so tricky to "count."

The strategy I used most frequently with office paper, *creating digital files,* has its pluses and minuses. Creating digital files reduces physical paper clutter, but it creates digital clutter in the process. Physically, this is a much neater form of clutter, but to some extent creating digital files simply displaces the problem since these files will likely require more of your time, energy, and attention somewhere down the road.

If you have a home office, culling through your office paper will evoke many useful reflections about your life: how you've spent your time, what you've accomplished that's worth remembering, and perhaps the occasional regret or two. Be prepared to encounter some valuable insights about yourself that are well worth revisiting.

Books — Ah, books... For the millions upon millions of people who love them, books are treasures by definition. Book lovers are fiercely attached to books; many of them treat books in their physical form as sacred objects, and some even regard the very smell of a book to be "one of the most wonderful scents in the world." Lots of book owners react with hostility or dread to the prospect of parting with their books; some of them find even the very idea to be unthinkable.

Clearly, letting go of books poses its own special set of challenges, and the process often requires using more advanced versions of thinning the herd strategies, such as these:

Designate a defined space for books. One way to cull a herd is to "pen the herd" by reducing or limiting the amount of available space for it. In my case, I decided that all of my books needed to fit into a floor-to-ceiling bookcase I'd installed in my home office. The bookcase had two rows of seven shelves each, about 45 square feet in all, which seemed like a reasonable amount of space for my book collection. Many of my books were located in several other standalone bookshelves scattered throughout the house, so it took quite some time and effort to consolidate this collection into the office bookcase, but eventually all my books fit there.

Having a defined space can also support more specific versions of thinning out a herd of books. A shelf of books is a logical and distinct location to choose for culling books one shelf at a time, and shelves are also easy areas to organize while you cull (in my case, it was by general topic on each shelf). This process often exposes books that don't seem to fit into any particular category, or into your life anymore for that matter. You might also do some *culling by association,* which happens when you're looking for one book and find yourself looking at another one, wondering why you still have it, and then deciding that there's no longer any reason to keep it.

Usually, weaker members of the herd will soon reveal themselves when you use these strategies. Do I *really* need a print copy of a thesaurus in this digital age? No (#1,135; donated). Or that old sudoku book with all the puzzles already solved? No one else will either (#1,408; recycled). How about those used, outdated college test prep books? Nope (1,673-1,676; recycled).

It's also easy to combine culling strategies with various gratitude strategies. Books are especially easy ways to **generate mutual gratitude** by giving them away either as gifts or donations and feeling good about it. Revisiting a book is also a worthy occasion to *retell* yourself one or more *stories* about what that book has meant to you: where you bought the book, when you read it, what great insight(s) it gave you, and so many more. You can even use the *time travel* strategy sometimes when rediscovering a long-forgotten book; remind yourself that your life was fine before you rediscovered this book and would still be fine if you decided not to keep it anymore. In each case, **expressing thanks** for the role that the book has played in your life also supports the culling process and helps you let go with gratitude.

Although I kept a sizable majority of my book collection, using these strategies enabled me to let go of a total of 78 books during my first and second projects. Going through my collection reminded me that books were a marvelous way to learn, to think differently, and to discover or imagine new possibilities, but that they could also be a way for me to hide from life if I let that happen or wanted to. Be prepared to discover similarly valuable things about yourself and your life as you sort through your collection of books and cull them.

Maps are not a special challenge for many people, but they were for me. Maps are one of my favorite paper things in life, and I was particularly attached to my collection of United States road maps, which I revisited during the second project. This collection was even more extensive than I'd remembered, consisting of over 200 maps. Most of them dated back to the 1960s and 70s when gas stations gave them away for free; the collection also included some state-issued road maps and a few other miscellaneous types. There were also a few other maps stored in various locations in my office and basement.

Maps were never easy for me to release, but I was able to thin out the herd by a dozen or so during the first project (#111-119, 130, 801, 962, 966, 977; recycled) and a few more during the second project (#1,544-1,545, #1,784-1,788, #1,834; recycled) by selecting damaged, out of date, or redundant ones. Even then, it surprised me that I had actually let go of any of them, and my US road map collection remained untouched, a designated treasure that I planned to keep.

Your Paper Life is not your real, everyday life, but it has a reality which offers its own rewards and treasures. If the written word has been an important part of your life, a huge chunk of your life's meaning is embodied and stored on paper, whether it's personal journals, books, office paper, or in some other form. The process of culling your paper possessions provides many opportunities to learn about what your Paper Life tells you about your whole life, and it's likely to involve surprisingly personal discoveries which await your experience.

Memento Territory

Sorting through your Paper Life inevitably takes you into memento territory. Mementos are objects you've kept specifically to remind yourself of a person or special event, and of course many mementos are in the form of paper: ticket stubs, concert programs, newspaper clippings, and photographs just to name a very few. Mementos by definition have a special value, but their value often changes over time, so using a combination of culling and gratitude strategies works well sometimes for sorting through collections of mementos.

For instance, one fall weekend, I found myself in a culling mood and so spent the better part of an afternoon going through boxes of mementos, letting most of them go (#1,749-1,848) by using a combination of culling and gratitude strategies. This included several trophies (#1,749-1,751, 1,771, 1,774-1,775; partly recycled, partly trashed), assorted art work (#1,799-1,803, 1,812-1,822; recycled) and packets of school work from my youth (#1,804-05, 1,823-1,832; recycled). Of course, remembering many stories was a natural part of the process, and I was moved to capture one or two of them in a blog post. Taking a lot of pictures also made the process easier, even though I was well aware in the moment that I would likely never look at the pictures again. It helped that many of the boxes and a few of the objects had a faintly moldy smell, such as my old high school tassel (#1,770; trashed), some Little League pictures (#1,833, recycled; #1,835-36, trashed), and a few road maps that were not part of my US road map collection (#1784-1,788; recycled). It felt a little sad to throw these out, but it also reminded me of all the moldy things in our parents' house that we had also reluctantly tossed.

Donation Culling

Using a combination of strategies is also helpful for parting with large numbers of items at one time, for example when doing donation culls. A donation cull is a process of collecting donation-worthy items over a period of time (weeks or even months) and then giving them en masse to a willing charity recipient. My donation culling process used the following combination of strategies:

Identify a suitable home. Using a donation center for getting rid of lots of unwanted things can feel like you're passing on your "too much stuff" problem to someone else, even if you're donating useful items. One way to address this concern is to set some guidelines to follow, such as these:

- Know in advance which items a donation center takes or doesn't take.
- Do your very best to meet their guidelines of acceptable items to donate.
- Find a donation center that accepts a wide variety of items.

Select objects of value. Use thinning the herd, picking out representatives, and other culling strategies to select objects for donation that others would value. For instance, the donation cull at the end of my second project included a number of useful household items which I hadn't used in many years, such as some placemats, a couple of serving dishes, some tablecloths, and a set of mason jars. I also had the luxury of including a few items with some possible monetary value that I no longer wanted, such as a crystal glass flower vase and a serving tray.

Gather items into a staging nest to make the donation process easier. In my case, the main staging nest was in the living room near the front door. Using a staging nest made it easy to box, count, and assure that appropriate items were included in a given donation.

Give with gratitude. A donation cull is an act of generosity, not purging. It feels better and more generous to give things away that might have real value for others. For instance, it felt good to give away a nice ceramic pitcher which had been in a box in the basement for well over a decade. It may have had special meaning for me once, but that meaning had passed. Better to let it go and find a home where it would start new stories and be better appreciated.

My first project included two donation culls, a very large donation (130 items) early on and a smaller one toward the end. During the second project, I did three donation culls; the last one was a large one that brought me to the end of the project (#1,943-2,033), which also meant that it was time to decide whether or not to do another project.

✾ ✾ ✾ ✾ ✾ ✾ ✾ ✾ ✾ ✾ ✾ ✾ ✾

Your Turn: Your Culling Habits

1) **Culling Strategies.** Use the table below to identify which culling strategies you have used for sorting through your tough stuff. For each strategy, list the items or collections for which you used this strategy and briefly describe how it worked (or not) for you.

Culling Strategy	What Collection(s)/Tough Stuff You Used This For	How It Worked/ Didn't Work
Thinning Out the Herd [or your name for this]		
Exterminating the Herd [or your name for this]		
Picking Representatives [or your name for this]		
Idea Mining		
Picking a discrete location or object		
Culling by shelf/spatial area		
Organizing while culling		
Sprints		
Designating a defined space "'pen the herd")		
Culling by association		

2) **Your Tough Stuff and Strategy Combinations.** What kinds of things are especially tough for you to let go of and why? What combination

of strategies have you used to get rid of some of your tough stuff? How did they work (or not) and why?

3) **Donation Culling.** What guidelines do you follow for doing mass donations? What combination of strategies do you use for preparing a donation? What else works (or not) for you when you do a mass donation and why?

Throwing Your Life Away: Letting Go of the Tougher Stuff

Time to Get Good at It: The Third 1,000 Things Project

Being strategic about the process during my second 1,000 Things Project had helped me build a healthier relationship with my stuff. Learning new strategies from others, tuning in to healthy talk, and turning culling into a habit produced some good results. My house looked and felt even less cluttered after all that culling; the kitchen, dining room, backyard shed, porch, basement, and closets were all noticeably clearer. Several nests were completely gone in the basement and dining room. My home office was almost under control, if not exactly tidy, and the volume of papers and items there had diminished considerably. One small file cabinet was entirely empty, as was one drawer of a second file cabinet. All the extra bins were gone, as were the stacks of papers from the storage carts. Tops of surfaces were almost clear. There were actual spaces on my bookshelf. Every area, box, or shelf of my house had been examined at this point, and there was little new left to discover. Occasionally I re-encountered a stash of forgotten things, such as a stack of music-related books stored inside the piano bench, but I was now aware of almost every thing I owned. On the intake side, saying "No, Unless" when deciding on new purchases had become a habit, and the flow of new things into my home had slowed to a trickle.

After all this progress, my ultimate goal of knowing the purpose or value of everything I owned felt noticeably closer, but it was still not in sight. So I decided to see if doing a third 1,000 Things Project would get me there. Once again, the project had a head start thanks to the 33 additional items from the donation cull at the end of my second project, but my house still held plenty of mementos and other challenging possessions to go through. I had gotten a lot better at letting things go, but now it was time to get good at it — really good.

Throwing Your Life Away

There's the tough stuff, and then there's the even tougher stuff.

Letting go of things which have been especially valuable or important in your life can be really difficult, even painful. A fellow writer of mine captured this feeling perfectly during a conversation at one of our monthly group meetings when she commented that trying to get rid of some of her things felt as if she was "throwing a part of my life away."

You might feel the same way about some of your stuff, as I did about some of mine. It's especially common to feel this way about mementos you've kept to remember a person or special event: *'I can't get rid of this; it'd be throwing a part of my life away!'* The very idea of sorting through our more treasured mementos can evoke the fear of losing something, of literally throwing away a piece of oneself to be lost and gone forever.

Fortunately, if you sort through your mementos and other tougher stuff with thoughtful attention, eventually you'll realize that you don't really *have* to keep *all* of them, and in fact you probably don't even *want* to keep some of them. You may hear an inner voice with a different message like this: *'I may think I'm throwing a part of my life away, but I'm not really. There are lots of good reasons to let some of these things go instead of holding on to them.'* Letting the tougher stuff go can be a lot less tough if you're strategic about it; you can transform the experience from a difficult, painful sense of loss into a rewarding, even enjoyable sense of gain.

Strategies for Letting Go of the Tougher Stuff

It can be tougher to let go of other things besides mementos for a variety of reasons. Some things are hard to get rid of not because they're important to you, but because they're unimportant, such as various kitchen utensils, unused items in your medicine cabinets, or manuals for appliances you don't have anymore. This is especially true with objects that don't take up a lot of space and are mixed in with items you do use, so it can take extra energy and attention to sort them out. Sometimes it's hard to decide whether something is still useful or worth keeping. For instance, you might have collections of items that you haven't used in a long time, such as kitchen gadgets buried deep in the back of a cabinet, gardening equipment stored in an outdoor shed, or recreational gear shelved in the garage, but you just might use them again. It can also be hard to find good homes for some things that you no longer need but don't want to just throw away, especially once being thoughtful about your belongings has become a habit.

The strategies that work with these other types of tougher stuff are familiar to you by now, and you can also use them in new combinations. For instance, you can start a donation cull by collecting worthy items and then looking for opportunities to give them away as individual gifts. Even simple things can generate mutual gratitude, and my staging nests held several items which found grateful recipients, such as a box of fire starter sticks (#2,442), a set of wind chimes (#2,443), and a cookie jar (#2,444). You can then complete the donation cull by donating any remaining items to charity. Of course, you will also encounter objects which are not donation worthy, and spending energy trying to find homes for them may not be worth it either. Throwing these objects away may be the best option, as I did with a set of nail files (#2,046), some plastic kitchen tongs, knives, and cups (#2,060-2,064), and some used spray paint stencils (#2,838).

Most often, though, more difficult items have been important to us, especially mementos. Tuning in to your healthy talk is a good place to start with these things. When you hear the messages telling you about the painful loss of "throwing your life away," listen also for the messages that enable you to revisit fond memories and remember stories about these objects. Each of your mementos will have a story to tell or often lots of them, as mine did. For instance, leafing through an old high school student handbook (#2,051; recycled) instantly evoked the images, sounds, and smells of walking down hallways between classes; reading the words to a school song reminded me of a rather less reverent version which my fellow marching band percussionists and I created and sang at (in?)appropriate occasions.

Adding one or more gratitude strategies to the process can help with more difficult items. For example, letting go of a corkscrew cover (#2,070) that was missing the actual corkscrew was harder than you might expect because it was a memento from a hotel in Northern California where my wife and I had stayed on our honeymoon. I needed to reminisce about our trip and take a picture of the object first before allowing myself to toss it into the recycling bin.

Developing a specific combination of strategies can also help with collections of mementos. For instance, here is a five-step combination of strategies I used to sort through from my college and early adulthood years:

1) *Revisit.* I went through each letter and reviewed its contents one more time as a form of thoughtful attention. Some letters invited longer, lingering visits, while only a brief moment was needed for others. I thoroughly immersed myself in the experience, so it took many hours to revisit them all, but it was time well spent.

2) *Remember stories.* I remembered, and in a few cases relived, the stories these letters told. It was surprising to remember how much writing we did back then in those pre-Internet, pre-email days. Our correspondence was often lengthy and detailed, even with people who were not especially close friends, but somehow this made the revisiting process easier by reducing the need to read every letter word for word. The remembering process revealed many discoveries, insights, and revelations. Most of the memories were fond ones, but

even the not-so-fond ones were worth remembering. A few of the letters offered some very personal recollections that I felt grateful to have rediscovered.

3) **Major cull: thin out the herd, pick representatives.** I saved a small enough proportion of the letters to fit into a shoebox, while I filled an entire recycling bin (#2,081; 2,179 - 2,195) with the ones I culled, which included hundreds of letters, cards, and a few pictures.
4) **Express thanks.** I recognized the recycled letters as objects that I no longer needed to keep, thanked them for reminding me of so many fond moments in my life, and then let them go with gratitude.
5) **Keep with gratitude.** My shoebox of letters was now a curated, manageable keepsake collection representing many memorable experiences that I could revisit anytime.

A few individual mementos also inspired me to capture stories about them. A pair of soccer cleats (#2,311; trashed) which I wore to play ultimate frisbee back in the day had particularly strong sentimental value. The cleats were at least 35 years old, and the dirt on them had been there for close to a decade; a cleat was missing, and one shoe had a tear on the side. I'd only worn them once in the past 20 years and didn't plan to wear them again, so there was no practical reason to keep them. I took a moment to recall fond memories of wearing them while playing ultimate on warm sunny Saturday mornings in the park, leaping in the air to make catches, and scoring goals in tournaments. Then I took a picture, wrote about them in a blog post, and let them go with gratitude.

Enough Is Enough: The Power of Satiation

The experience of sorting through mementos for a sustained period can also actually make it easier to let things go.

This may sound counterintuitive at first, especially if the process of going through your mementos occasionally re-triggers your fear of throwing your life away. If that happens, going back to basics helps; tune

Throwing Your Life Away: Letting Go of the Tougher Stuff

in to your healthy talk, look and listen for the stories your mementos have to tell, and allow them to fill you with remembrances again. As you revisit your mementos for a sustained period, most likely you will eventually experience a very different reaction: allowing your mementos to fill you with their remembrances produces a feeling of **abundance** instead of emptiness.

This happened to me when I went through my old personal writing journals. I'd saved decades' worth of them with the idea that some of their contents might be useful Some Day, so it was worthwhile to go through all of them and at least glance at each page, looking for insights about my past thoughts and what resonated with me now. There were a few insights that were worth rediscovering, but mostly the ones I found no longer served their purpose. After a while, the revisiting process filled me with lots of satisfying memories until I reached the stage where enough was enough, and this sped up the process of going through the remaining writings. After revisiting them all, I did a major cull (#2,445-2,446, #2,599, #2,912; recycled), letting them go with gratitude for the journeys of my "interior life" and the many treasures they had provided along the way. Even if a useful insight or two was lost in the process, I had already collected more than enough of them.

Sometimes you might find yourself keeping most of what you sort through, and that's OK; after all, most of your mementos were once treasures, and some of them may still be. You may not be ready to let go of some things just yet, or ever for that matter. In most cases, though, you're likely to find that using a combination of letting go strategies helps you revisit mementos one more time, remember their role in your life, and then let most of them go with gratitude, keeping a small representative sample to remind you of the larger collection.

You may also discover that experiencing the power of satiation is a familiar strategy as well as an effective one, because in fact you've already been using this strategy your entire life. The reality is that most of the stuff you've owned in your life is now long gone and forgotten. After all, even the most adept of collectors don't keep everything they accumulate as they go through life, and even if you tried, eventually you would reach the limits of your capacity to remember experiences by accumulating things. Can you remember every beautiful landscape or artwork you've seen, every wonderful person you've met, every clever remark you've heard or made, every great meal you've enjoyed? Of course not. It's simply impossible to keep a memento or other recollection of every single memorable experience in your life. (Many people would need a small Smithsonian-like Museum Support Center to house their collection.)

This reality applies just as much to the things you still own. Your collection of mementos represents only a small portion of your life experiences, and sorting through them is really a process of negotiating the size of that collection. This size will differ for each person, but if you've ever felt that you have too much stuff, odds are that your relationship with your stuff will be healthier if your collection of mementos is smaller.

This was how my experience of going through my mementos went. Eventually I realized that there were more than enough of them and that it was OK to get rid of the rest. It felt better to have fewer and be able to enjoy them than to keep so many that their value and meaning got lost in the shuffle. It was satisfying to know that I could fill my need to remember without having to fill my basement, spare rooms, or a storage unit with stuff. Even looking at the list of those things I no longer owned was more satisfying than still having them stored away and forgotten in some box in the basement. Your relationship with your stuff becomes much healthier when "enough is enough" — when you no longer need to keep everything you have and are satisfied by what you keep.

The Power of Mementos

There's something magical about re-encountering a long-forgotten object from one's past. Mementos remind you of things you once did but had

Throwing Your Life Away: Letting Go of the Tougher Stuff

forgotten you were even capable of doing. They allow you to rediscover insights, power, or truth that was once important and that might even be useful to reclaim. The memories can be harsh at times, reminding us of what we once had, knew, or were, and especially of what we've lost. But they can also remind us of the many treasures of good living: hard-won lessons, wonderful adventures, or challenges overcome that have made us wiser, better people. You did wonderful and sometimes great things, and you can keep on doing them in the future.

Going through my mementos gave me one especially pertinent insight. During my second project, I found paper copies of a differential aptitude and general interest test that I took in eighth grade (#1,713; scanned/recycled). One particular result on the differential aptitude test caught my eye: a 99th percentile score for a category called "clerical speed and accuracy." Reading this reminded me of how deep and long-standing my clerical streak actually was. It certainly helped explain the exercise and diet logs (#2,715-2,726, 2,731-2,739; scanned/recycled), the work task management logs (#2,740-2,744; scanned/recycled), and the various other notes, logs, and similar documents which I encountered later. On my general interest profile, the computational category had the highest score out of 10 categories, while literary was third and clerical was fourth, all of which were higher than the musical, scientific, and mechanical categories among others. Hmmm — computational, literary, clerical? Perhaps I was destined to do these 1,000 Things Projects and write a book about them.

This is the power of mementos: to give you the experience of connecting your past to your present, strengthening the value and purpose of each. This is what your things can tell you if you listen, whether you hold onto the physical thing or not. Mementos are worth the extra time, energy, and attention it takes to go through them. The process of culling mementos to a small representative collection can actually bring them back to life and reveal a truly liberating truth: that having a healthy relationship with your stuff depends not on how much stuff you can keep, but on how much stuff you can appreciate.

✻ ✻ ✻ ✻ ✻ ✻ ✻ ✻ ✻ ✻ ✻ ✻ ✻

Your Turn: Letting Go of Your Mementos and Other Tougher Stuff

1) **Throwing Your Life Away.** Name one or more of your possessions that made you feel as if you were throwing your life away. What did you decide to do with it and why?

2) **Your Strategies for Letting Go of Tougher Stuff.** Identify one or more strategies or combinations of strategies you've used to let go of some of your mementos or other tougher stuff. How well did they work (or not), and why?

3) **Enough is Enough.** How have you used the power of satiation to help you let go of mementos? Which strategy or strategies did you use? How did it feel when you reached that point of "enough is enough"? How did this experience affect how you dealt with some of the other things that you own?

Appreciation: The Healthiest Habit

A Healthy Appreciation

The best way to build a healthy relationship with your stuff is to appreciate it.

Appreciating your stuff can take many forms. It can be a form of *gratitude or thankfulness,* such as the feeling of being grateful for what you have or as an act of expressing that gratitude. Being able to *understand fully your situation,* in particular to *understand the true nature of your relationship* with your stuff and to *realize why it's important* to you is another way to appreciate your stuff. You appreciate many of your more treasured possessions by having a *sensitive awareness of their aesthetic qualities or values.* Appreciation also refers to an *increase in price or value* of an asset; investments such as houses and other real estate, stocks, or precious metals can all appreciate, and the same thing happens to your stuff when you appreciate it.

All of these forms of appreciation connect you with the touchstones of building a healthy relationship with your stuff. Respecting the power of possession helps you fully understand the true nature of your relationship. Engaging in healthy talk with your belongings helps you gauge its importance to you. Being mindful about bringing new things into your life reflects a healthier understanding of how you want to live.

There are many healthy ways of appreciating your stuff, such as feeling or expressing gratitude for stuff you're letting go, experiencing the beauty or meaning of your treasured possessions, or increasing the value of your things by remembering their stories or by culling your collections to a manageable size. This connection with the touchstones of building a healthy relationship with your stuff is why appreciation is the healthiest habit of all. At first, this appreciation may take the form of a simple feeling or passive awareness that remains largely in the background, as it did for me during my first 1,000 Things Project. But as with all habits, having a healthy appreciation needs to be something that you actively do. This can be an overt action, such as telling someone you are grateful or capturing a story about one of your possessions. More broadly, this action takes the form of the time, energy, and attention that you put into developing your relationship with your stuff.

When you're strategic about the process, appreciating your stuff becomes a practice, which is the key to getting good at it. You can take your practice to the next level by using familiar strategies and trying out new ones with the intention to seek, find, generate, and spread appreciation. With regular practice, appreciating your belongings eventually becomes a habit and moves into the foreground of your relationship.

Any of the strategies described in this book can help you develop the habit of healthy appreciation. There are also some strategies you can use to focus more directly on developing this habit. Here are a few of them that worked for me.

Tapping the Power of Display

Storing away valued items is a curation strategy that works well for keeping things out of sight and mind but not very well for appreciating them. Re-engaging with valued items that you've kept in storage for a long time will eventually make you question why you still keep them in places where no one can appreciate them, especially yourself.

One way to get good at appreciating your stuff is to ***tap the power of display*** by selecting some of these valued objects, taking them out of storage, and putting them on display in your home. I used this strategy to create a display with some of my valued possessions that were small enough to fit on my living room mantelpiece. This collection of display items included a large pine cone from a memorable hike in California during my honeymoon, some intriguingly shaped deer vertebrae that I found on a mountain near where I grew up, and some large conch shells collected from Florida beaches a half century ago when they were still abundant.

Being able to hold, touch, or simply look at a valued object provides a sense of happiness, pleasure, and even aliveness. Putting treasured objects on display instead of keeping them stored in boxes in your attic or basement gives you many more opportunities for these moments of appreciation — pausing to recall a fond memory, reflecting on the passage of your life, or sharing those stories with others. Displaying treasured objects enables you to appreciate them more, and in turn, your treasured objects appreciate in value when you display them.

Creating displays is also a great strategy for helping you let go of things because displays also tap into the power of satiation. For example, deciding to put the conch shells on display prompted me to thin out my remaining collection of shells and throw a bag of them away (#1,852). After taking several serving bowls out of storage and putting them on display, I felt fine about giving away two other serving bowls (#2,351-2,352; donated) since I could better appreciate the ones that remained on display. I never missed the shells or serving bowls once they were gone, and displaying them dampened my desire to collect more of them.

Your displays of prized possessions represent an even greater storehouse of the good times and fond memories you have been fortunate to experience. They can be a constant source of satisfaction which you can access with a simple, brief glance. Spending a little more time with them can induce that feeling of satiation where you realize that what you already have is enough.

Appreciating Privilege

Another way to get good at appreciating your stuff is to appreciate the privilege of having it. Encountering my personal "treasure trove" during my first project raised questions for me about the relationship between the project and my affluence. Practicing the habit of healthy appreciation eventually answered these questions by making me realize that being able to appreciate my stuff derives from a position of privilege.

This word has become a loaded term for some people, so it's worth describing the meaning of privilege in this context and its connection with appreciation. Appreciating your privilege is all about understanding your situation by recognizing that having stuff is not a given, a birthright, or something to be taken for granted, but rather a "benefit, advantage, or favor" that is not available to everyone. For instance, it helped me to recognize that the collections of things I valued and enjoyed were not available to me when I was younger and less affluent.

This privilege comes in several forms, such as accumulation, abundance, and affluence. Being able to accumulate things at all is a privilege not available to countless numbers of people living in the world today. Being able to have more stuff than you need is another obvious form of privilege. Being able to put voluntary limits on what you own is perhaps a less obvious one; that is, it's a privilege to be able to go through your stuff and decide what to keep and what to let go, keeping only what you want and getting rid of excess, knowing that you can always get more if you want. The process of doing a 1,000 Things Project is thus itself a form of privilege.

Affluence enables other forms of privilege, such as being able to select more expensive, longer lasting, higher quality items rather than choosing what you own mainly on the basis of price. Affluence affords the privilege of having a greater variety and volume of choices, of being able to buy goods, services, and experiences for personal growth or pleasure, and of coordinating your purchased possessions into a neatly curated design which reflects you and your lifestyle.

Appreciating our privilege also means exercising our choice about what to do with this privilege. We can choose to simply ignore our good fortune and enjoy its benefits, or we can recognize and respect the

Appreciation: The Healthiest Habit

responsibility that comes with the power of privilege. Being responsible starts (yet again!) with paying thoughtful attention to the things that we own and learning how to use the freedom that affluence brings to make better, more respectful choices. We can practice active charity to others by giving away the material things we don't need. We can practice self-charity by reducing our need to be surrounded by material things and easing the burden of their possession in the process. We can be respectful to the planet by being mindful about the things we choose to own and about how we dispose of them. Choosing to exercise responsibly the privilege of having stuff thus also helps us build a healthy relationship with it.

Spreading Appreciation: The Tool Cull

One of the best ways to get good at appreciating your stuff is to spread that feeling around. I did this at the end of my third 1,000 Things Project by collecting my tools and doing a massive cull of them. I figured that my tools would be more useful if I actually knew where they were and owned far fewer of them, so I decided to sort through them all, keep enough useful ones to fill two toolboxes, and give away the rest.

Immediately this decision stirred a choir of inner voices: *'Have you SEEN how many tools there are?' 'Isn't sorting through ALL of them a bit much?' 'Aren't you being just a LITTLE compulsive about this?'* That stopped me for a moment until I remembered my Dad's tool collection. He had at least seven toolboxes filled with tools and a huge amount of tools that weren't in toolboxes. He also had numerous toolboxes filled with all sorts of things that weren't tools, such as the ones filled with the rolled-up pennies organized and labeled by year. In comparison, I only had two toolboxes plus various other tools loosely stored in several other places, but I was still young relative to my dad when he passed away. *'Maybe he only had as many tools as I do now when he was my age. Maybe he got started down the path of tool collecting with just two toolboxes.'* That thought quickly prompted a healthy change of script: "Better for me to cut down my own collection now while it is still manageable in size." That alone was enough to justify my decision to sort all the tools.

And so I did. I emptied my two toolboxes and collected all the other tools I could find, laid them out over a large area, grouped the tools loosely by type, then started identifying those that I wanted. If there was only one of something I wanted, it went into the first toolbox; if there were two of them, the second one went into the second toolbox, and anything left over stayed in a third pile. Even after filling two toolboxes, a fairly useful collection of leftover tools remained: a couple of hammers, various screwdrivers, pliers, and a wide assortment of wrenches, including an almost complete socket wrench set. Some of these were new or almost new, such as a set of ratcheting wrenches, while others were older but still useful, such as an old Yankee screwdriver and a small metal plumber's wrench, which I kept in the giveaway pile figuring the recipient might appreciate these 'vintage' tools more than I would.

Then I bought a new plastic toolbox at the local hardware store, filled it with the culled tools, and added a separate bag with a funnel and some boxes of nails, screws, and other fasteners. The resulting package (#2,923-3,008) was a very popular offering on Freecycle and quickly found a recipient. I even got a response from someone who didn't want the tools but simply wanted to acknowledge my generosity:

> Hi neighbor, Very generous tool freecycling you have got going there! I am not really in need but I thought I would let you know I think that is a pretty cool gift.

The tool cull was a great way to finish my third 1,000 Things Project because it reflected how I had gotten good at appreciating my stuff. I gave away things I no longer needed much more freely and generously. Negative self-talk no longer stopped me, even when sorting through the hundred-plus items in my tool collection. It was gratifying to find a good home for these tools and imagine them finding new value and purpose while releasing myself from the burden of possessing them. The tools I

Appreciation: The Healthiest Habit

kept appreciated in value and purpose now that they were stored in one location, easy to find and use more frequently. I quickly forgot about the tools I gave away and didn't miss any of them.

Once you reach the point where spreading appreciation becomes second nature, chances are that your relationship with your stuff is a healthy one, or at least a much healthier one than when you started your journey. Practicing a healthy appreciation for your stuff will help you sustain this as an ongoing relationship, and getting good at appreciating your stuff will repeatedly remind you of how this relationship is personal.

Your Turn: Appreciating Your Stuff

1) **Healthy Appreciation.** How do you appreciate your stuff in healthy ways? Use the table on the next page to:
    - Identify which forms of healthy appreciation you have for your things;
    - For each form of appreciation, identify an item you've kept and describe how you appreciate it; and/or
    - Identify an item you let go of and describe how you appreciated it when you had it; if applicable, also describe the appreciation you generated by letting it go.

2) **Tapping the Power of Display.**
    - Identify one or more of your possessions that are on display in your home or other place. How do you feel when you look at this object?
    - Identify an object that you have recently taken out of storage and put on display. How did you feel when you did this? How do you feel when you look at the object now?
    - If you haven't done this recently, find an object that you have in storage, take it out, and find a place to put it on display. How do you feel when you do this?

Forms of Healthy Appreciation	How You Appreciate Something You Kept	How You Appreciated Something You Let Go
Feeling gratitude or thankfulness		
Understanding the true nature of your relationship with your stuff		
Realizing why the relationship is important to you		
Having a sensitive awareness of their aesthetic qualities or values		
Increasing their value or worth to you		
[list other forms of healthy appreciation here]		

3) **Spreading Appreciation.** How have you spread appreciation? Which strategies did you use? How did it feel after you were done? How did this experience affect how you dealt with some of the other stuff that you own?

Part V: Getting Personal

Building a Long-Term Healthy Relationship...and Beyond

Distinctively Yours

Your journey to build a healthy relationship with your stuff is a personal one. Your experience of the elements which are common to all these journeys will be distinctively yours — your process, your strategies, your results — and all the more so if you've been doing a 1,000 Things Project your way. Your project(s) will likely have at least somewhat different goals from the ones that I or others have chosen. You will also use the strategies in this book differently from how other people have used them; you'll use some of them more often, some less, and some not at all.

You may also use other strategies which weren't a part of my journey but may become a part of yours. For instance, you might use *helpers* to go through your stuff with you. Using helpers can support your efforts in several ways, such as helping you plan and do stuff-sorting sessions, offering encouragement as needed, or providing a second opinion on decisions about individual items. You might use a different method, such as the ones described in the Learning from Others chapter or one that you discover on your own, such as **death cleaning,** a decluttering method which encourages older people to get their physical possessions in order before they die so that their things won't be a burden to their children or others.

You might also find yourself in circumstances that force the issue of getting rid of stuff, often in ways that are not so thoughtful or strategic. Moving is probably the most common event that forces the issue. The moving process usually shortens the time you have to figure out what to do with all of your stuff, so it speeds up the decision-making process. While some people avoid this issue by putting some of their possessions in a storage unit, even then the moving process leaves less time to sort through stuff than you might like. Other major life events, such as marriage or divorce, can also force the issue of dealing with your things (and often someone else's stuff as well) by making it necessary to purge your own stuff, merge them with someone else's stuff, or separate your stuff from someone else's. Although it can feel liberating to be rid of a relatively large proportion of one's stuff, more often forcing the issue results in people feeling sadness or regret from missing many of the things they lost or chose to leave behind.

Your experience of what works or doesn't work will also be distinctively yours. For instance, you may find that being generous with giving away things comes more easily to you than it did for me. You might be able to set daily numerical targets and meet them while still being thoughtful about the process (which I was never able to do for more than a few days at a time). You might find that staging nests help you to speed up the process. You are also likely to use different strategies and have different results when dealing with the inevitable slogs you encounter, which will happen because every relationship journey has its ups and downs.

Yours for the Long Term

Speaking of which, how *is* that relationship with your stuff going these days?

I hope it's going well for you because, as you know by now, you're in a lifelong relationship. So long as you own stuff, your relationship with it will last. This relationship is not going away, so why not make it a healthy one for the long term?

Good long-term relationships with people are healthy ones: strong, meaningful, powerful, helpful, fulfilling. Doing a 1,000 Things Project can help you build and maintain an ongoing, healthy relationship with your stuff for the long term in many ways, such as these:

- *Being thoughtful about the process* of dealing with your stuff helps you connect with your reasons for having it.
- *Being strategic about the process* helps you build powerful habits for getting good at it.
- *Turning your inner dialogue into healthy talk* helps you make thoughtful decisions about what to do with your stuff.
- *Recognizing that you're in charge of the relationship* enables you to decide what to keep and what to let go, what to value or use and what to release for others to use.
- *Keeping the things with clear value and purpose* is a much more rewarding use of your time, energy, and attention than keeping things which have lost their value and purpose to you.
- *Letting go of things you no longer want or need* helps you feel at ease with the things you no longer possess without a sense of loss or regret.
- *Becoming mindful about acquiring new items* helps you have less stuff without feeling deprived and increases the value of the items you do decide to acquire.
- Simply *having, using, and wanting less stuff* is healthier because:
  - Being satisfied with having and keeping fewer things helps you appreciate them more fully, knowing that they are a representative sample of your life stories and experiences;
  - Opening up physical, mental and emotional space makes it easier to find stuff when you need it and to live your life without having your stuff get in the way.
  - Wanting less stuff gives you much more control over your life than feeling so possessed by needing more stuff that what you have is never enough.

Building a Long-Term Healthy Relationship...and Beyond 153

- *Appreciating your stuff* is the healthiest habit of all because it connects you with all the other ways of building a healthy relationship with it.
- *Spreading appreciation* by *using the power of generosity and gratitude* to create appreciation in yourself and others through giving things away is a clear sign of a healthy relationship.
- *Appreciating your privilege* and exercising it responsibly helps you practice the habits that support your healthy relationship.
- *Doing the process your way* personalizes your experience, because after all it's your life and your relationship.

Anyone who does a 1,000 Things Project can experience these benefits, and your experience of them will become more personal as you actively seek them by doing your project(s) strategically.

Your experience of these common benefits, and the changes you experience as the result of your journey, will be distinctively yours. Some of them may be more meaningful, powerful, or fulfilling to you than others, and the strength or importance of each may change over time, which is a part of your ever-changing relationship with your stuff.

An Ever-Changing Relationship

Changing Goals: A Receding Horizon — Building a long-term healthy relationship with your possessions changes the relationship over time. For instance, your goals may change, even the ones that got you started in the first place. This happened to me with my ultimate goal of knowing the purpose or value of everything I owned. After finishing my third 1,000 Things Project, it seemed as if reaching this goal was finally in sight and that making a "punch list" of the remaining tasks would get me there. The punch list was fairly long, a combination of about three dozen items and related tasks. I figured that I could get through the list fairly quickly by applying what I'd learned from my previous projects, so I set a deadline of eleven weeks to complete it. After eleven weeks, many of the list items were completed, but many more remained; in fact, it took much longer to get rid of some of them, and the entire list of items was never actually finished.

Doing the punch list didn't take me to my "ultimate" goal, but it gave me something far more important. It taught me that my goal was an illusion, a receding horizon, always in sight but never to be reached. Knowing the purpose or value of my stuff was not a destination; it was part of the journey, an integral part of building a healthy relationship. Falling short of this goal was not a sign of failure, but was actually a sign of a relationship that was healthy and ever-evolving.

Changing Values: A Healthy Evolution — This evolution happens because the value of the things we own changes over time. Many of them lose their purpose or value; they become unnecessary as pastimes or hobbies or other life circumstances change. Building a healthy relationship with your stuff accelerates this evolution in several ways. Having fewer things helps you appreciate what you keep, but that also raises the bar of expectations for the items that you still have. It's as if your remaining stuff is now exposed and no longer has a place to hide, which calls the purpose or value of less appreciated items into question. Feeling more satisfied with what you have also reduces the need to have so many items; it lowers the value of keeping things simply for the sake of keeping them.

As a result, even once-treasured items can lose their value. In my case, a box of memorabilia from my youth which was identified as a treasure during my first project was culled during the second project; only a few representative examples of school papers and sports team pictures remained. My parents' grandfather clock became a gift to a relative for him and his family to enjoy. Eventually, I even donated my road map collection to a road map collectors' organization.

Changing the Basics: A Place Beyond Counting — Your most basic strategies can change over time as well. For instance, a 1,000 Things Project is built on counting, but you may reach a place where counting no longer serves you. This happened to me after my third project. As I continued getting rid of things, eventually I lost track of the exact number and realized that there was no longer a need to keep counting just for counting's sake. Even though the effort to count had clearly been worth it up to that point, I had arrived at a place beyond counting, one where building and maintaining a healthy relationship with my stuff no longer depended on counting how many items I let go of. So I let go of counting as well, knowing that it was always available to me whenever I wanted to use it again (which in fact I did some time later).

Uniquely Yours: A Journey Beyond Stuff

Your relationship journey reaches an entirely new place when the changes you experience along the way start to change you.

Relationships change people. Whenever you work on building a healthy relationship, sooner or later you're no longer the same person you were when you started: the relationship changes you. Some of these changes are expected or even planned, such as the ones resulting from reaching the goals you set, while other changes can take you to places where you never expected to go, transforming your journey from a distinctive experience to one that is uniquely yours.

These changes that go beyond your relationship with your stuff are the most personal of all, and they become a departure point for changes in your life that may be surprising, unsettling, or even life-transforming. In my case, I began calling this changing point "the unraveling" after reading a quote by Brene Brown which was posted on a social media site:

> People may call what happens at midlife "a crisis." But it's not. It's an unraveling — a time when you feel a desperate pull to live the life you want to live, not the one you're supposed to live. The unraveling is a time when you are challenged by the Universe to let go of who you think you are supposed to be and to embrace who you are.

My unraveling was neither midlife nor crisis, but it was a coming apart of sorts. My 1,000 Things Projects started this unraveling process by creating physical, mental, and emotional spaces in my life. Getting rid of so many things thoughtfully helped me resolve many of the intricacies, complexities, and obscurities embodied in my relationship with my stuff, clearing up some old mysteries and revealing new possibilities in the process.

As this unraveling moved beyond my relationship with my stuff, it began to involve broader changes in other aspects of my life by enabling me to loosen knots or tangles and to start disengaging myself from them. I unraveled my relationship with televised media by "cutting the cord" altogether, that is, discontinuing my cable television service without substituting any streaming or other services. I gave up car ownership altogether and started building a new relationship with my transportation needs. Being mindful about buying less stuff completely unraveled my sense of being someone who, based on my stage and place in life, could accumulate lots of stuff more or less whenever I wanted.

This unraveling also deepened my ability to appreciate my status as an entitled consumer and the privilege that enabled me to do all this, including the privilege of choosing to have less stuff and the privilege of having a level of consumption that most other people don't have. Thinking about how to use my privilege took me far beyond deciding what to do with an old shirt in my closet or a kitchen appliance that I no longer used much. I began to explore how I might tread more lightly on the earth so that less fortunate others could have something more. The thread connecting my individual consumer decisions and their global impacts became more real and visible once I unraveled it.

As I began to redefine some of my identities, such as cable television viewer, vehicle owner, and entitled consumer, my unraveling became both a pull and a release towards living the life I wanted to live, not the life I was supposed to live.

Cutting the cable cord freed up lots of time which I spent instead on exploring some new activities which had always interested me but which I'd never focused on before. In place of channel surfing in the evenings, I started taking improv and acting classes. Using an online language program helped me brush up on my Spanish and learn more French, and I also started taking classes at a nearby fitness studio. Instead of spending time on the weekends watching televised sports, I took more hikes and bicycle rides during the day and went to improv practices and performances in the afternoons and evenings. Unraveling my cable viewing habits also helped me free myself from limiting beliefs, such as the ones that said I could never do acting or learn a new language or run faster. Not every hour I saved was spent productively, but I got much better at managing the time I spent on social media or online surfing.

Giving up car ownership enabled me to learn a different way to meet my transportation needs. I got into the habit of walking to nearby places where I would have reflexively driven to previously. When walking wasn't practical, using a combination of bicycling, public transportation, car rentals, and ride share services filled my transportation needs almost all of the time. Figuring out how to use my time productively on longer public transit trips became an engaging challenge. Being less dependent on a vehicle for transportation supported healthier habits, reduced my carbon footprint, and increased my awareness about other areas of my life where my behavior could be less reflexive as well.

Acting more like a conscious consumer than an entitled one created yet another virtuous cycle. More awareness gave me time and energy to explore ways to remove more attachments to consumer goods, products, and brands that I didn't really need, which in turn led to more thoughtful, less reflexive choices.

As I continued to redefine these ways of being in the world, my unraveling became a journey unto itself. New identities emerged along the way that I never would have imagined for myself when my first 1,000 Things Project began: actor, improviser, triathlete, citizen activist. I found myself wondering what else would happen as a result of making space for yet more unraveling — but that is another story..

❈❈❈❈❈❈❈❈❈❈❈❈

Your Turn: It's Always Your Turn

Wherever you are on your journey to build a healthy relationship with your stuff, you can always take a moment to step back, reflect on what you've accomplished, and appreciate how you have changed as a result. So, who are you now? Where has your journey taken you, and how has it changed you?

It's possible that doing your 1,000 Things Project(s) wasn't really much of a personal journey. Maybe your project was a simple decluttering exercise that didn't focus on your relationship with your stuff. As a wise friend told me, "Clutter is a word devoid of any relationship," so if your project focused on clutter control, then it probably didn't change you much at all, which is fine. After all, a 1,000 Things Project is something that you do your own way, so if your sole goal was to have less clutter in your home by getting rid of 1,000 things or whatever number you chose, I hope that you've reached your goal(s) and that you feel good about the results!

If, however, you focused on thoughtfully building a healthy relationship with your stuff, chances are that your process has moved way beyond a simple decluttering project, and your journey has become a personal one. Your journey may have helped you to (re-)discover the deeper, more meaningful, even sacred connections that you have with many of the things you possess, and so you may well know your stuff a lot better now than when you started.

You may also have a deeper appreciation of how you've changed as the result of your journey. You may now have become someone who:

Building a Long-Term Healthy Relationship...and Beyond

- Knows how to use the downsizing process to help you age with intention, move to a new dwelling, or otherwise move on with the life you want to live;
- Realizes that taking care of your stuff is a way of taking care of yourself;
- Wants to do good by giving away your belongings to others in need;
- Knows how to slow down the flow of objects into your life that you don't want or need;
- Is exploring how having less stuff can help contribute to healing the planet;
- Is much more aware of the importance of your relationship with your possessions as the result of living through a pandemic; or
- Simply wants a long-term, healthy relationship with your stuff.

However you've changed and whomever you've become, I hope that you like the results, and I hope that reading this book has helped you along the way. Your stuff is an extension of you; it lives through you, and you live through it. Your relationship lasts as long as you do, and your journey to have a healthy relationship with it is a lifelong one that will give you an abundance of joy, satisfaction, and appreciation for the privilege of having stuff to enliven your journey through life. Thank you for reading this book, and enjoy the journey!

Acknowledgements

This book is the product of hundreds of conversations with friends, colleagues, and family. I wish to thank in particular those colleagues, friends, and others who helped me refine many of the specific ideas presented in this book or who have helped me share those ideas with others: Monica Adler Werner, Wendy Anderson, Hilmir Ágústsson, Jenny Apostol, Alice Bedard-Voorhees, Emily Boehler, Jeff Boehler, Suzanne Brown, Louann Carlan, Lisa Cheney-Steen, Jewell Dassance, Beth Davis, Katharine Dow, Denise Easton, Candice Falger, Dave Falger, Esther Geiger, Steve Gilbert, Peggy Goetz, Lisa Goodwin, Sheryl Hansen, Patti Jennings, Jan Keller, Eric Krathwohl, Kenneth Langer, Merrill Leffler, Donna A. Lewis, David Lindrum, Christine Lustik, Candiya Mann, Joan McMahon, Leslie Mason, Mary McCaffrey, Sarah McCaffrey, William McCaffrey, Cynthia McCourt, Mindy McWilliams, Bodil Meleney, Michelle Mentzer, María Ölversdóttir, Veronica Palladino, Marika Partridge, Sam Pinkerton, Dale Pike, Jan Poley, Julie Porosky Hamlin, Michelle Procansky-Brock, Larry Ravitz, Judy Redpath, Jeff Richards, Rob Rosenbalm, Claudine SchWeber, Joanne Scribner, Chris Sener, Patricia Sener, Joel Snyder, Jeffrey Stein, Sara Taber, W. Allen Taylor, Jody Telfair-Richards, Jen Tyler, Peggie Weeks, Trish Weil, Mary Wells, Mary Wild, Kari Wiliford, Mary Wissemann, Jenn Sorika Wolf, Jeremy Wolf, Lukas Wolf, Susi Wyss, Mike Young, and Missy Young.

Special thanks to my colleagues who reviewed the manuscript and provided helpful feedback: Jim Beane, Ed Bowen, Nicole Damour, Lynn Dohm, Kathleen Fulton, and Wendy Gilbert. Also, special thanks to Beth Baker for providing her skillful editorial touch to the manuscript. Extra special thanks goes to the Republic of Writers Group, whose enthusiasm for the topic helped bring this book into being. Thanks also to you, the reader, for reading this book. I hope that it has been worth your while.

Notes

Part I: Getting Started

You and Your Stuff:

aging with intention: I first heard this phrase from the Washington Ethical Society, which has an Aging with Intention Group that meets regularly to discuss topics related to aging. Also see: https://ethicalsociety.org/connection/small-group/aging-intentions-group/

Beyond Clutter Control:

I got out a piece… end of the calendar year: I started the project on May 7, so it was actually 239 days through December 31, but setting a deadline was more important than the exact number of days.

130 boxes of stuff: A colleague who had moved at around the same time told me that his move involved about 400 boxes in addition to the unboxed stuff. I had a lot fewer things to move, but 130 boxes still seemed like a lot of stuff to me.

didn't have lives of their own exactly: The belief that inanimate objects can have their own life force has a long history in cultures throughout the world, for instance the life energy concepts of chi (China), ki (Japan), and prana (India), or the Maori concepts of mara and mauri (see The Encyclopedia of New Zealand, https://www.teara.govt.nz/en/te-ao-marama-the-natural-world/page-5). In Western cultures, modern scientific thought has largely rejected the belief that matter is alive in some sense (a philosophical system called hylozoism; see https://www.britannica.com/topic/hylozoism), although many attempts have also been made in science and philosophy to re-embrace this belief (see https://en.wikipedia.org/wiki/Hylozoism).

Getting Started:

seek a tax credit: Consumer Reports offers a handy guide for getting tax credits for donated items which is updated yearly: https://www.consumerreports.org/taxes/tax-deduction-on-donations/

Ten Thousand Things: From the *Tao Te Ching* by Lao Tzu. The ten thousand things are mentioned in many chapters of this classic book, for instance Chapters 1, 2, 4, 5, 8, 25, 32, 34, and 62.

pretty easy to get rid of 1,000 things: One solution to this problem is wittily depicted in this *New Yorker* cartoon; Roz Chast, "The Life-changing Magic Of Shoving Everything," *Conde Nast Store*. Retrieved from: https://fineartamerica.com/featured/the-life-changing-magic-of-shoving-everything-roz-chast.html.

fell behind schedule: based on a rough mental calculation of how many things needed to go each month in order to reach my goal by the end of the calendar year.

Part II: Holding On

Stories:

actual metal objects: This strategy would serve me well on many occasions later in the project.

geographic origins of the pencil: The geographic origins of the pencil apparently continue to be of interest. A National Geographic learning activity describes a more recent geography of a pencil: https://www.nationalgeographic.org/activity/geography-of-a-pencil/

Inner Voices:

scripts: In psychological theory, scripts are a type of schema, i.e., knowledge structures that describe the typical sequence of events in common situations. We use scripts in social situations (for instance greeting people or ordering food in a restaurant) so that we can use prior knowledge to help us anticipate the future, set goals, and make plans. For instance, see Rohini Radhakrishnan, "What Are the Four Types of Schema in Psychology?" MedicineNet, February 9, 2021. Retrieved from: https://www.medicinenet.com/what_are_the_four_types_of_schema_in_psychology/article.htm

The Psychology Dictionary offers a more formal definition: a "mental representational format which outlines the basic actions needed to complete a more complex action." http://psychologydictionary.org/script/

mantras: Popular culture has expanded the original meaning of the word into a broader meaning of "a word or phrase that is repeated often or expresses someone's basic beliefs." http://www.merriam-webster.com/dictionary/mantra

Always get the lowest price! This mantra, of course, is also the foundation of the big box retail industry.

internalized rules and messages: Advice about saving and scrimping and getting Maximum Value for one's purchases pre-date the Depression, of course, but internalizing my parents' Depression experience through the lessons that they had passed on to me was the main source for my Maximum Value mantra.

inner critic's negative self-talk: For instance, see: Jennice Vilhauer, "4 Ways to Stop Beating Yourself Up, Once and For All," *Psychology Today*, March 18, 2016. Retrieved from: https://www.psychologytoday.com/blog/living-forward/201603/4-ways-stop-beating-yourself-once-and-all.

Treasures:

"store of valuable or delightful things": https://www.google.com/search?q=trove+definition&ie=utf-8&oe=utf-8

Scientific American article about birds' nests: Nina Bai, "Treasure in the Trees," *Scientific American*, vol. 305, no. 2, 2011, pp. 66–67. Retrieved from: http://www.scientificamerican.com/article/treasure-in-the-trees/ [subscription required]

cleaning one up: For nests that were less visible, such as those in the basement or in closets, cleaning one up still made a noticeable psychological difference because I could compare how the area looked before and after my efforts and feel satisfied by the difference.

Possession:

many meanings of the words "possess" and "possessed": http://dictionary.reference.com/browse/possess?s=t

Total Cost of Ownership: In accounting terms, the Total Cost of Ownership (TCO) refers to the purchase price of an asset plus operational costs. The TCO of owning a car, for instance, is the purchase price plus the expenses incurred through its use, such as fuel, repairs, and insurance. For more details, see Alexandra Twin, "Total Cost of Ownership — TCO," Investopedia, July 28, 2020. Retrieved from: http://www.investopedia.com/terms/t/totalcostofownership.asp

whether these costs were large or small: For example, I could tell you from memory the purchase price of every house I'd ever bought, but I didn't know the total payoff amount for any of them without looking at the mortgage documents.

Vampire devices: http://www.pcmag.com/encyclopedia/term/60226/vampire-device

Vampire power: John Schueler, United States Department of Energy, "Are Energy Vampires Sucking You Dry?" Breaking Energy, October 30, 2015. Retrieved from: https://breakingenergy.com/2015/10/30/are-energy-vampires-sucking-you-dry/

Phantom load: the Lawrence Berkeley National Laboratory, more prosaically, calls this "standby power:" http://standby.lbl.gov/

equates to about an hour per day: Or 57.6 minutes to be more exact, assuming 16 hours of waking time per day.

This family is in deep trouble: Well, that's not what the family members who were present then told me when I asked them about it some years later. But I suspect they were just being polite.

Part III: Letting Go

Curation:

largest museum and research complex in the world: Smithsonian Collections Media Fact Sheet, August 1, 2018. Retrieved from: https://www.si.edu/newsdesk/factsheets/smithsonian-collections

over 2.7 million square feet of display area: "Smithsonian Museums Now Mapped from the Inside Out," The Smithsonian Institution, July 10, 2012.

Retrieved from: https://www.si.edu/newsdesk/releases/smithsonian-museums-now-mapped-from-the-inside-out

pinhole photo: David Schloss, "Massive 3,000 square foot pinhole photo on display," *DP Review*, May 2, 2014. Retrieved from: http://www.dpreview.com/articles/4558111479/massive-3-000-square-foot-pinhole-photo-on-display

less than two percent of the 155 million objects: Smithsonian Collections Media Fact Sheet, August 1, 2018. Retrieved from: https://www.si.edu/newsdesk/factsheets/smithsonian-collections

larger than what is depicted in the movie: The Smithsonian is also far more careful about keeping track of what it has.

America's Attic: for example, see:
- Kate Armstrong, "Exploring America's attic: a guide to the Smithsonian Institution," *Lonely Planet*, April 15, 2004. Retrieved from: http://www.lonelyplanet.com/usa/washington-dc/travel-tips-and-articles/exploring-americas-attic-a-guide-to-the-smithsonian-institution-in-washington-dc
- Edward Rothstein, "At the Smithsonian, America's Attic Is Ready for Its Second Act." *The New York Times*, November 21, 2008. Retrieved from: https://www.nytimes.com/2008/11/21/arts/design/21hist.html; and
- Michael Kernan, "A Real Nation's Attic," *Smithsonian Magazine*, November 1997. Retrieved from: http://www.smithsonianmag.com/history/a-real-nations-attic-146080337/

"the increase and diffusion of knowledge": Smithsonian Institution, "Purpose and Vision" web page. Retrieved from: https://www.si.edu/about/mission

decision fatigue set in: Decision fatigue refers to a person's decreasing ability to make decisions resulting from the emotional and mental strain of having to make many decisions. There is some controversy about what decision fatigue actually is or whether or not it's avoidable, partly as the result of a lack of a common definition for the term. For me, decision fatigue was a real phenomenon which I experienced whenever I became overwhelmed with a volume of decisions I had to make. See, for example, Jon Johnson, "What Is Decision Fatigue?" *Medical News Today*, July 6, 2020 (retrieved from: https://www.medicalnewstoday.com/

articles/decision-fatigue) or Cindy Lamothe, "Understanding Decision Fatigue," *Healthline*, October 3, 2019 (retrieved from: https://www.healthline.com/health/decision-fatigue).

a tiny fraction of the donations that are offered to them: For more details about the Smithsonian Institution's selection process, see the Smithsonian Institution Archives Reference FAQ, Donations and Donors section. Retrieved from: https://siarchives.si.edu/what-we-do/reference-faq

nowhere near as involved as curating a museum collection: Museum acquisition and collection management policies are very involved; for example, see the Wikipedia entry on museum collection management policies (retrieved from: https://en.wikipedia.org/wiki/Collections_management_(museum)) or the J. Paul Getty Museum Collection Policy (September 15, 2019; retrieved from: http://www.getty.edu/about/governance/pdfs/acquisitions_policy.pdf)

my job was to oversee their care: For instance, here are curator job descriptions from the University of Rochester (retrieved from: http://mag.rochester.edu/plugins/acrobat/teachers/MuseumCareers.pdf) and TotalJobs.com (retrieved from:https://www.totaljobs.com/careers-advice/job-profile/education-jobs/curator-job-description).

interrelated meanings: For instance, compare these entries from the Online Etymology Dictionary:
- Definition of cure (retrieved from https://www.etymonline.com/search?q=cure);
- Definition of curative (retrieved from https://www.etymonline.com/search?q=curation);
- Derivation of curation (retrieved from https://www.etymonline.com/search?q=curative).

basic definition of culling: to choose; select, pick; from: http://www.dictionary.com/browse/cull

culling the herd: This expression commonly describes the process of removing weaker or undesirable members, for instance: https://idioms.thefreedictionary.com/cull+the+herd. It is also used to describe the process of controlling the size of an animal population, for example: https://

www.merriam-webster.com/dictionary/cull. Sometimes, an entire herd is exterminated, for instance to prevent the spread of disease: https://www.collinsdictionary.com/us/dictionary/english/cull

picking something out for a reason: http://www.thesaurus.com/browse/cull

Thinning out the herd: In retrospect, I'd used this strategy even before I'd started the 1,000 Things Project, in particular when I culled the five bags' worth of pencils, crayons, and other writing tools, which were part of the first 70 items I got rid of (#53-63, 66-70; Freecycled). Labeling the strategy helped me use it more consciously during the later part of the project.

Gratitude:

Kenner building sets: One Bridge and Turnpike, one Girder and Panel.

VAC-U-FORM: A Mattel VAC-U-FORM was a device that enabled users to create their own plastic toys by using molds of various items and melting a sheet of plastic on an exposed hot plate.

Slow on the Inflow:

wasn't as much stuff coming into my home: This was due to my own changing habits and my son having gone off to college.

being thoughtful about getting rid of my existing stuff…being more mindful about buying new or used stuff: Although the words *thoughtful* and *mindful* overlap in meaning (for instance, both refer to being attentive or aware), *thoughtful* often refers to the act of being considerate (https://www.dictionary.com/browse/thoughtful), while *mindful* often refers to the act of being careful (https://www.dictionary.com/browse/mindful), as in "minding what you're doing." The "No, Unless" strategy introduced an element of minding; saying "No" first required me to mind my decisions and make them carefully instead of mindlessly. So for me, thoughtful attention was more about being considerate of the things I already had, while mindful attention was more about being careful about acquiring new things (although also see the next chapter for how I also experienced the other main meaning of mindfulness).

occasional mindless purchase: For instance, while shopping for other clothes on one occasion, I bought a couple of pair of shorts, thinking that I might wear them for weekend cookouts, but then I hardly ever went to any, and I ended up never wearing those shorts either.

The Results:

clearly useless junk or otherwise not worth saving: For instance, there was a bag of trash from the car (#109), a shower curtain with some black spots on it that wouldn't wash out (#754), a bottle of long expired ear drops (#924), a truly disgusting toilet brush (#927), and decades-old toilet paper found in a camping backpack (#933), to name a few.

throwing away 50 CDs inflated the total: I trashed these at the county recycling center after finding out that they were not recyclable, contrary to what I'd read online. Also, I counted each CD as one thing since I had gone through them one by one to decide whether or not to keep any of them.

a form of mindfulness: This form of mindfulness related to the psychological technique of observing one's experiences as distinct from mindfulness as being carefully attentive. Also see https://www.dictionary.com/browse/mindful for these respective definitions.

state of active, open attention to the present…awakening to experience: https://www.psychologytoday.com/basics/mindfulness

heightened awareness…non-judgmental: https://www.merriam-webster.com/dictionary/mindfulness

labor-saving devices: https://www.reference.com/history/labor-saving-devices-bb08d8fc07c1e1ba

Part IV: Getting Better, Getting Good…

Starting a Second Project:

how to be strategic: Some readers might note that the distinction I'm making here is more one of strategy (a set of goals and plans to achieve them) vs. tactics (specific actions designed to accomplish a strategy). However, I have not used the words *tactics* or *tactical* in this book because I never thought in these terms during my projects, and I also wanted to avoid any military connotations which might imply that such an approach is an essential part of doing a 1,000 Things Project. You, of course, are free to use the terms and to be tactical about your project as you like.

practices and habits: *practice* implies intention, that is, a conscious repetition of an action or activity to improve skill, while *habit* describes an action performed automatically, usually without awareness. Also see this definition of the distinction between the two: https://wikidiff.com/habit/practice

Learning from Others:

possessions might burden her children when she passed away: We had this conversation before either of us had heard of "death cleaning" (see the Getting Personal chapter for more details about this approach).

five books to read:
- Marie Kondo, *The Life-Changing Magic of Tidying Up: The Japanese Art of Decluttering and Organizing*. Berkeley: Ten Speed Press, 2014.
- Julie Morgenstern, *SHED Your Stuff, Change Your Life: A Four-Step Guide to Getting Unstuck*. Touchstone, 2011.
- Kate Evans Scott and Melinda K. Bryce, *Letting Go: The Tao of Decluttering*: K.L. Press, 2015.
- Melva Green and Lauren Rosenfeld, *Breathing Room: Open Your Heart by Decluttering Your Home*. Atria Books/Beyond Words, 2015.
- Bea Johnson, *The Zero Waste Home: The Ultimate Guide to Simplifying Your Life by Reducing Your Waste*. Scribner, 2013.

weigh you down: If the clutter is "weighing you down, crowding you out, blocking your light, cramping your style; if it's become an obstacle you keep stumbling over...if it's stopping you from finding the things you really love, then it's time...to let it go." (*Breathing Room*, p.2)

Zero Waste included useful sections: Chapters 2, 3, and 4 were particularly useful in this regard.

detailed checklist: This checklist was also a helpful referral list for letting go of items throughout the house, although it was too detailed for me to use with every item I encountered.

narrow criteria: The books I read used a variety of criteria for defining the meaning of one's stuff, for instance joy (*Tidying Up*), joy and purpose (*Letting Go*), purpose and ease and love (*Breathing Room*), or what you truly use, need, and love (*Zero Waste*), but my criteria of purpose and value allowed me to define a broader range of values as meaningful to me.

do decluttering in sprints: see Vicki-Lynn Brunskill, "sprint (software development)," *TechTarget SearchSoftwareQuality* (retrieved from: https://searchsoftwarequality.techtarget.com/definition/Scrum-sprint), for a detailed description of how sprints are used in agile software development.

Tuning in to Healthy Talk:

a familiar inner voice: This was, in fact, the same inner voice that kept a large plastic bin (#600; donated) at my house for so long

ski trainer: In the case of the ski trainer, I'd tried to sell it first without success, so I also had to use another new script to let it go: "It's not worth the effort required to recover its monetary value, and even if it was, giving it away is more satisfying than selling it."

Thank you for the role you have played… This script was derived from *Tidying Up* and from *Letting Go*.

We can treasure [this person, place, memory]… This script was derived from the stories that several of my friends told me about their similar experience with this.

Figure out how much time I am saving… This script was derived from my own project experience and enhanced by the example from *Letting Go* (see Learning from Others chapter for related quote).

Culling as Habit:

"**one of the most wonderful scents in the world**": Piotr Kowalczyk, "30 book-scented perfumes and candles," September 11, 2017. Retrieved from: https://ebookfriendly.com/book-smell-perfumes-candles/. Explains why, despite an ever-growing landscape of e-books, there are over 30 different book-scented perfumes, candles, and sprays, but of course nothing can ever really replace the scent of a book itself.

floor-to-ceiling bookcase: The bookcase was installed prior to my 1,000 Things Projects, but it came in handy for helping me stick to this strategy.

all my books fit there: That is, they fit if I stacked books on top of books within each shelf, but at least they were all now in one defined location.

a total of 78 books: I got rid of 39 books during each project. For the first project, 16 of them were donated (#909-923, 1000), 14 were gifts (#95, 786-798), and nine were recycled (#98, 854-856, 928-931, 951). For the second project, 27 were donated (#1,002-1,006; 1,135-1,141; 1,199; 1,561-1,570; 1,669-1,672); six were gifts, (#1,719=1,724); and six were recycled (#1,405; 1,408; 1,673-1,676).

remind yourself of a person or special event: https://dictionary.cambridge.org/us/dictionary/english/memento

passing on your "too much stuff" problem: As also described in the **pretty easy to get rid of 1,000 things** footnote above.

following this set of guidelines: These suggestions may sound like simple common sense to many people, but they are often not followed. To be honest, I did not know or follow all of them either when I started my projects; I had to learn some of them along the way. See for example, Editorial Board, "Please, don't donate trash to charities," *Rochester Democrat and Chronicle*, April 2, 2018 (Retrieved from: https://www.democratandchronicle.com/story/opinion/2018/04/03/dont-donate-trash-charities/467065002/)

Throwing Your Life Away:

filled an entire recycling bin: Mementos like this one also posed the issue of how to count them. Each individual letter required some time, energy, and attention, but I would have finished the entire third project just by counting each letter as one thing and then still have had a lot left to do. As a result, I used the boxes they came from (11 in total) as my unit of "thingness" and counted each picture (7 in total) as a single thing. Again, this was self-defined and somewhat arbitrary, but the contents of each box varied enough to require a shift of attention, and, most importantly, this decision worked fine for my purposes.

Appreciation:

Appreciating your stuff can take many forms: This paragraph refers to several definitions of appreciation as described in the footnotes that follow.

a form of gratitude or thankfulness: https://www.thesaurus.com/browse/appreciation

the feeling of being grateful: https://www.macmillandictionary.com/us/dictionary/american/appreciation

ability to understand fully the true nature of your relationship…and to realize why it is important: https://www.macmillandictionary.com/us/dictionary/american/appreciation

sensitive understanding of their aesthetic qualities or values: https://www.lexico.com/en/definition/appreciation

increase in price or value: https://www.bankrate.com/glossary/a/appreciation/. These last two definitions derive more directly from the original meaning of the word, which refers to the act of setting a price or estimating the quality of something: http://www.etymonline.com/index.php?term=appreciation.

all about understanding your situation: As in this definition of appreciation: https://www.lexico.com/en/definition/appreciation.

"benefit, advantage, or favor": https://www.merriam-webster.com/dictionary/privilege

not available to everyone: https://www.lexico.com/en/definition/privilege

exercising our choice: The first step involves recognizing the variety of sources from which one derives one's privilege. See, for example, Point #7 in Maisha Z. Johnson, "What Privilege Really Means (And Doesn't Mean) – To Clear Up Your

Doubts Once and For All," *Everyday Feminism*, July 21, 2015. Retrieved from: https://everydayfeminism.com/2015/07/what-privilege-really-means/.

giving away the material things we don't need: In addition to Freecycle, there are other local groups which I discovered after completing my projects which can help you give away material things you don't need. For example, Buy Nothing (https://buynothingproject.org/) is an organization which aims to enable local groups of people to create a gift economy by creatively and collaboratively sharing their abundance, including material things they don't need.

fill two toolboxes: The second toolbox was intended for my son in case he wanted it; if not, it would be easy to give away to someone else.

anything left over stayed in a third pile: I also kept a separate toolbox for myself which I had taken from my dad's tool collection and kept because it had a well-organized array of tools (socket wrench set, a few screwdrivers, tool bit disk, and a few other items) that wouldn't all fit in my toolbox.

a new plastic toolbox: You may recall that I'd given away a toolbox during my first 1,000 Things Project (#599) because I didn't need it at the time, so you might wonder if I felt some regret for not having kept it. In fact, the opposite happened: buying the new toolbox reminded me that giving away the old toolbox had felt more rewarding than keeping it even if I might need one again Some Day. In fact, I gave away the new toolbox after deciding that I actually liked my old ones better. Giving away the new toolbox also expanded my feeling of generosity, which made it seem like a relative bargain for the price.

Part V: Getting Personal

use other strategies...different method: There are several common ways to get rid of things that I never used during any of my projects, including yard sales, consignments, or "curb alerts" (discarding unwanted items by putting them out in my front yard next to the curb and then posting a message online for anyone to come and take them). Although I tried to sell a few items by consignment or on Craigslist, I never actually sold any of the 3,000+ things that I got rid of.

helpers: Many people told me that having helpers was very useful, but I never used one during my projects.

death cleaning: The definitive book on death cleaning is Margareta Magnusson, *Dostadning: The Gentle Art of Swedish Death Cleaning*. Canongate Books, 2017. Retrieved from: https://canongate.co.uk/books/3192-dostadning-the-gentle-art-of-swedish-death-cleaning/. I never used this method since I didn't learn about it until after I'd finished the 1,000 Things Projects.

Other major life events: During the 1,000 Things Projects, several people told me stories about losing possessions as the result of natural disasters, which also force the issue in even more unpleasant ways. One was from a fire, in which the family lost almost everything from their home; another was the result of a flooded basement which ruined lots of their possessions that had to be thrown out. There was even one from a lightning strike (!), which forced the family to throw out about 25 bags of clothing and to get all of their remaining clothing dry cleaned.

a coming apart of sorts…intricacies, complexities, and obscurities: These observations are based on the two main definitions of unraveling: to *disentangle, disengage,* or cause the separate threads of something to come apart; and to *find the correct explanation* for something, to *clear up* (for instance, to unravel a mystery) or to *resolve the intricacy, complexity, or obscurity of something*. (See http://www.merriam-webster.com/dictionary/unravel for these definitions.)

These notions of unraveling can be good or bad depending on the circumstances. Unraveling as describing something that's failing or beginning to fail is bad when something is coming undone that we wanted to keep together or did not want to fail, such as a sweater, a ball of yarn, or a marriage, but it's good when we're untangling something that we want to untangle, such as electrical cords, shoelaces, or a relationship in transition. Unraveling as clearing up a mystery or finding the correct explanation for something sounds good, but we might not always like what we find as a result.

living through a pandemic: this section was written during the COVID-19 pandemic.

Appendix: Chart of Strategies

The tables on the following pages provide an extensive list of strategies for building a healthier relationship with your stuff.

Strategy	Description	Works best/helps with...
The Master Strategies		
Be thoughtful	Everything starts with being thoughtful by paying thoughtful attention.	Everything
Time, energy, and attention (TEA)	Commit to spending the time, energy, and attention you need to do your project.	Everything
Do It Your Way!	Your goals, your ground rules, your timeline	Everything
Getting (Re-)Started Strategies		
Know Your Goals	Identify your goal(s) and how you will know when you've reached them	Getting started; energizing the project with purpose
Personalize your project	Give your project a name; choose your target number; set your own timeline	Getting started; generating energy and enthusiasm
Start with easy stuff	Start any session by identifying and removing the easiest things first. (This is also a culling strategy.)	Things that are ready for removal; ones that are clearly trash; easy targets in nests, other collections
Culling Strategies		
Go through/cull by category	Go through your stuff by category (e.g., clothes, books, mementos, etc.)	Collections with a discrete type of item (e.g., clothes)

Strategy	Description	Works best/helps with...
Go through/cull by spatial area	Go through an entire spatial area (e.g., corner of a room, closet, shelf of boxes, etc.) or two at a time	Collections with a discrete type of item (e.g., clothes)
Red/Yellow/ Green	Sort an area, collection, or container by quickly identifying which objects to keep (red), which to get rid of (green), and which are not (yet) sure (yellow)	Any area or collection of things; good strategy for managing attachments
Thin out the herd *Variations:* **Pen the herd** **Organize and cull** **Cull by association**	Reduce collection to a manageable size by picking out "weak" items that are easier to let go. Reduce or limit the amount of available space for a collection. Organize an area while you're thinning out a herd or otherwise culling it. Question why you have an object (e.g., book) while looking for another one; decide not to keep it	Nests; collections with no easy stuff, such as clothes and books Collections with lots of items (e.g., clothes, books) Collections that are easy to organize (e.g., books) Sorting/culling by category
Exterminate the herd	Get rid of a collection completely.	Entire collections of things you don't really need
Pick representatives	Sort through collections, pick out a representative sample of things that you value, and let the other ones go.	Collections of mementos
Idea mining	Extract original ideas, insights, and other valuable nuggets from documents; throw out the remainder.	Paper files, other documents

Appendix: Chart of Strategies

Strategy	Description	Works best/helps with...
Pick a discrete location or object	Select a specific bin, file cabinet drawer, or other location or object.	Paper stuff; tackling a specific area
Creating digital files	Scan physical documents and convert them to digital form.	Office paper, photographs, other paper documents.
Donation culling	Collect donation-worthy items over a period of time, then give them to a willing charity recipient.	Donation-worthy items; giving away lots of items at once
Other Curation Strategies		
Consolidated storage of collections	Consolidate collections of stuff into a few identifiable storage areas.	Things you want to keep for now but deal with later
More open storage	Store things on open shelving, in clear or translucent bins, or in nests out in the open.	Things you want to keep for now but deal with later
Gratitude Strategies		
Generate mutual gratitude	Give things away that someone else can use or appreciate.	Things that you don't need or use but others might
Remember/ retell stories	Remember a story about an object, tell it to yourself silently or out loud; share it with others if appropriate.	Things you can release after one more revisit
Capture stories	Write down the stories which tell why you held on to the object.	More difficult items

Strategy	Description	Works best/helps with…
Take pictures	Take pictures or videos of something.	Things you don't need but might want to remember
Time travel	Go back in the past, before (re)discovering the object; ask yourself if you were OK then & would be OK now without this object.	Mementos you've just rediscovered
Express thanks	Recognize an object as something you no longer need, thank it for the role it has played in your life, and then let it go with gratitude.	Mementos, books, other (once) treasured objects
Enough is enough	Tap the power of satiation by allowing your mementos to fill you with their remembrances until "enough is enough" and you're satisfied with letting them go	Mementos, other (once) treasured objects
Slow on the Inflow Strategies		
From "Yes, if…" to "No, unless…"	Change your 'default setting' from "**Yes**, buy it **if** I want it" to "**No** need to buy something **unless** I really must have it".	Making decisions about buying new stuff
Tuning in to Healthy Talk Strategies		
Activate the storytelling	Ask yourself questions about that object and listen for the answers, e.g., when and where you got it, how you've used it.	Having trouble hearing the stories your stuff has to tell you

Appendix: Chart of Strategies

Strategy	Description	Works best/helps with...
Change the script	Convert scripts with outdated, questionable, or bad instructions into healthy ones by integrating gratitude, culling, or other strategies for letting go.	Any items, but especially more difficult ones
Find a new script	Write a new one; listen for a new one; gather them from other sources.	More difficult items
Practice healthy self-talk	Talk to yourself in a healthy way by comparing your progress with your goals, telling yourself simple affirmations, acknowledging negative self-talk when it happens, and externalizing some of your internal dialogue by journaling or other means.	More difficult items, but really any items
Appreciation Strategies		
Display your treasures	Select valued objects, taking them out of storage, and putting them on display in your home.	Things you want to keep and appreciate by having them visible
Appreciating privilege	Understand the forms of privilege that come with having stuff instead of taking it for granted; make responsible choices about using this privilege.	Appreciating your stuff
Spreading appreciation	Actively seek to create appreciation in yourself and others by giving things away or other actions	Creating appreciation in yourself

Appendix: Chart of Strategies

Strategy	Description	Works best/helps with…
Process and Other Strategies		
Count and Record	Count and record the objects as you remove them from your home and your life; provides an easy structure to the process.	Managing the process
Learn from Others	Collect ideas, tips, and strategies from friends, reading books, and other sources.	Process strategy
Decluttering as therapy	Focus on using a decluttering session to help you feel better about the process and the results.	Keeping it fresh by changing the focus
Remove the guilt	Detach the object from the person who's associated with it.	Items inherited from family members/other loved ones
Mix spatial and categorical sessions	Sort through your stuff by spatial area one session, then by category the next one.	Keeping it fresh by creating variety
Have a succession plan	Identify things that specific recipients will inherit when you pass away.	Valued items that you want others to have eventually
Helpers	Get a simpatico friend or relative to help you with the process.	Process strategy

Strategy	Description	Works best/helps with…
Sprints	Use bounded time periods (e.g., daily, hourly) focused on getting rid of a certain number of things in that time period, e.g., six things in one hour, 10 things in two hours, 15 things in one day, etc.	Bins, nests, and stacks of office folders
Pay thoughtful attention to being strategic	Figure out which strategies you are already good at (what, when, how often); which strategies are already practices and habits; which ones you could do more often, more effectively; keep discovering new strategies	Getting better at the process of being strategic
Your strategies	[Add strategies that you've tried and worked for you!]	Whatever works for you

www.ingramcontent.com/pod-product-compliance
Lightning Source LLC
Chambersburg PA
CBHW051434290426
44109CB00016B/1546